Border Bandits, Border Raids

W. C. Jameson

LONE
STAR
BOOKS

Guilford, Connecticut
Helena, Montana

LONE STAR BOOKS

An imprint of Globe Pequot
An imprint and registered trademark of Rowman & Littlefield

Distributed by NATIONAL BOOK NETWORK

Illustrations by Pee Wee Kolb, courtesy of W. C. Jameson

British Library Cataloguing in Publication Information available

Library of Congress Cataloging-in-Publication Data available

ISBN 978-1-4930-2834-4 (hardcover/paperback)
ISBN 978-1-4930-2835-1 (e-book)

♾™ The paper used in this publication meets the minimum requirements of American National Standard for Information Sciences—Permanence of Paper for Printed Library Materials, ANSI/NISO Z39.48-1992.

CONTENTS

Introduction

IN GLORIFYING AND PRAISING THE US MILITARY, MAGAZINES AND BOOKS have often pointed out that this country has never been invaded by a foreign power, or anyone else for that matter. This position has often been voiced at Memorial Day rallies, Veterans of Foreign Wars gatherings, and other patriotic assemblies. Praise for this stated accomplishment has been manifested and national pride for such expressed for decades, but it is not true. The United States has, in truth, been invaded on numerous occasions by foreign military and bandits, and the results were often disastrous.

The Mexican armies of Generals Pancho Villa and Venustiano Carranza conducted several cross-border raids, ostensibly to procure arms, ammunition, supplies, and food. In addition, Mexican bandits—sometimes organized and sometimes spontaneous—undertook raids into American settlements along the border leaving death and destruction in their wake. Such raids, and there were many, were responded to by the US military and the Texas Rangers as well as local, county, and state law enforcement agencies. Retaliation raids into Mexico by the US Cavalry and Texas Rangers were not uncommon.

The concept of a border varies with culture. Some cultures perceive a border as a firmly established line, a boundary, across which one may not pass unless equipped with specific authority or permission to do so. Citizens of the United States for the most part perceive a border in this manner.

Boundaries between states and counties are respected and honored as a result of this tradition to the degree that the regions circumscribed by such boundaries will manifest their own rules, regulations, politics, cultures, and social systems. Though neighbors, the United States and Mexico could not be more different in how they perceive the border separating the two countries.

To those steeped in Mexican culture, a border is simply a line. It can be a fence, a river, or a pen mark on a map, but it does not hold the authoritative energy and power for them as it does Americans. When a Mexican arrives at a border, he crosses it without a second thought simply because his destination happens to be on the other side.

This difference in philosophy has created numerous tensions and difficulties between the two nations for nearly two centuries.

Life along the US–Mexico border during the last half of the nineteenth century and the first three decades of the twentieth century was sometimes fraught with danger. Mexican nationals often crossed the border to steal cattle and horses from American ranches. In the process, men on both sides were often killed and wounded. Likewise, a number of prominent cattle ranches in Texas were initially stocked with cattle stolen from Mexico during acquisition raids.

When incursions from Mexico became more common and threatening, reinforcements were called in the form of the US Army and the Texas Rangers. These forces were intended to serve as deterrents, but following particularly aggressive and violent raids, the agents often became involved in aggressive pursuit and punishment. Results were mixed. The US military was initially ill equipped to deal with the rugged terrain of the border country from the West Texas desert-mountain region all the way down the Rio Grande to the Gulf of Mexico. Men and horses suffered and commands proved futile until their leaders could get their bearings and gain sufficient knowledge accumulated from experience. By the same token, the enemy, in the form of Mexican nationals, had lived and thrived in these environments for thousands of years, were well adapted to terrain and conditions, and were natural guerrilla fighters.

What they lacked was numbers, and in time the US military simply overran and wore down the opposition by virtue of superior numbers and armament.

The early Texas Ranger bands proved to be a clear threat and danger to the Mexican communities along the border. In spite of the heroic portrayals of the Rangers, many early commands were composed of riff-raff assemblages of thugs, murderers, and thieves. There exist numerous accounts of Ranger companies that indulged in illegal border crossings, executions, theft, and rape. Following several instances of such activities, the Rangers accomplished little more than exacerbating racial tensions along the border.

The Plan of San Diego was not much help in settling the concerns of those living along the border. This so-called plan, drafted by the head of Mexico's pre-constitutional government Venustiano Carranza and his agents in 1915, was intended to overthrow the US administration in Texas, New Mexico, Arizona, and California, to establish an independent Mexican-American republic on the lands that had been seized by the American government in 1848. A principal objective of the plan "called for an army consisting of Mexicans, Mexican-Americans, Blacks, and Japanese to kill all whites over the age of sixteen and the creation of a black republic in six southern states as well as the restoration of tribal Indian lands."

Many Mexicans embraced the Plan of San Diego. Others simply used it as an excuse to raid and pillage and exact revenge. During the many years of border difficulty, at least thirty raids from Mexico into Texas resulted in the destruction of millions of dollars in property, the stealing of thousands of head of livestock, and the killing of at least twenty-one Americans. Raids into Mexico by the US military, the Texas Rangers, and local posses resulted in the killing and wounding of dozens of citizens.

The following pages contain accounts and details of seventeen significant border raids with origins from both sides of the line. In addition to the violence and the subsequent involvement of the military and politics, the raids spawned a number of colorful characters—Mexican and American—that have since secured their place in history. None of these personalities, most of them outlaws, ever reached the legendary and international status of Billy the Kid, Jesse James, Butch Cassidy, and others, but along the US–Mexico border the names Chico Cano, Pancho Villa, Cheno Cortina, John Flynt, and others were often on the lips of residents far and wide, and are still whispered today.

CHAPTER ONE

The Night Raid of Cheno Cortina

JUAN NEPOMUCENO CORTINA WAS BORN IN CAMARGO IN THE MEXICAN state of Nuevo Leon on May 16, 1824. He was nicknamed "Cheno." During 1846 as the war between the United States and Mexico raged, Cortina moved with his family across the Rio Grande into Texas to an *estancia* that belonged to his widowed mother. A few miles northwest of Brownsville, it was called Rancho del Carmen, but Cortina referred to it as Santa Rita.

Under the provision of the Treaty of Guadalupe Hidalgo—February 2, 1848—Cortina became an American citizen. Cortina has been described as intelligent, handsome, well mannered, of medium height, with a light complexion, reddish-brown hair, gray-green eyes, and "a striking red beard." Though shrewd and competent, Cortina remained illiterate his entire life, and only learned to sign his name when in his fifties. Because of his red hair, he was sometimes referred to as "The Red Robber of the Rio Grande."

During the late 1840s, a Puritan merchant from New England named Charles Stillman opened a trading center near Fort Brown, which was located almost directly across the Rio Grande from Matamoros. A small settlement grew up next to the fort that boasted a few stores, a church, several cantinas, and sporting houses catering to the soldiers. After the war ended, business between the United States and Mexico grew at a rapid pace. As a result, land prices surged. A number of northerners who had served with the Army during the war decided this region would be a good place to do business dealing in land. Culturally, this was not a good fit, for the Yankees looked upon native Mexicans, as well as Mexican citizens of the United States, with contempt.

A number of the newcomers squatted on land owned by heirs to the extensive de la Garza holdings that were in and around Fort Brown, ownerships validated by the Treaty of Guadalupe Hidalgo. Stillman, in an attempt to obtain title to these lands, filed suit against the heirs, but the court disallowed it. In response, Stillman appealed the verdict and retained the law firm of Basse and Horde to offer thirty-three thousand dollars for a clear title to the land that he began referring to as "Brownsville."

Not eager to pursue litigation because of the cost as well as the growing feeling that they would lose, the de la Garza heirs accepted the offer. The title to the land was signed over to Stillman, who immediately declared bankruptcy. As a result, not a penny was paid to the heirs but, according to the law, Stillman was allowed to retain possession of the land.

Seeing how the courts favored the Anglos at the expense of the Mexican citizens of Texas, more land deals were negotiated by the newcomers, the majority of them characterized by fraud, trickery, and intimidation. Within a few short years, most of the lands along the border in this extreme southern part of Texas now belonged to the northern businessmen.

Cortina, whose property was six miles northwest of Brownsville, observed the illegal machinations and because of them, came to detest the Yankee traders. While his bitterness grew, he remained busy operating his own ranch, fighting off occasional bands of raiding Indians, and occasionally venturing into Mexico to steal cattle to bring back across the river and place on his own lands. While regarded as genteel and polite, Cortina rarely engaged with the citizens of Brownsville, preferring instead to ride the range with his cowhands.

Over time, Cortina had run afoul of the law on several occasions, but he was never arrested or charged with a crime. For a time, Cortina was a business partner for a man named Adolphus Glavecke. Glavecke

Juan Cortina

had arrived from Germany and established a successful ranch located between Cortina's and Brownsville. During the spring of 1859, Cortina and Glavecke had a disagreement over some cattle. Glavecke turned to Sheriff James Browne for help, providing the lawman with evidence against the rancher sufficient to indict Cortina for rustling one steer and one cow. After conferring with Cortina, however, Browne indicted Glavecke for receiving stolen cattle. In the end, neither man was arrested, but hard feelings and bad blood dominated their relationship thereafter.

On July 13, 1859, Cortina was drinking coffee at the Brownsville cafe of Gabriel Cachel when Marshal Robert Shears stepped through the doorway. Shears was described as "hulking" and a "bully." Shears stepped over to a small table where sat an elderly Mexican who was clearly drunk. Shears called the old man a spic, and ordered him to go with him, that he was to be arrested.

The old man was too inebriated to understand the meaning of the sheriff's words, so the lawman seized him, yanked him from the chair, and threw him onto the floor near the doorway. Stepping up to the prone victim, Shears cursed the Mexican and ordered him to get up. When the old man staggered to his hands and knees, Shears kicked him hard in the ribs, knocking him once again to the ground.

Initially, Cortina observed the sheriff's actions with contempt. When the bullying sheriff began to kick the old man, however, Cortina approached him and explained the old man was too drunk to respond, and that if it was necessary for him to go to jail then he, Cheno Cortina, would carry him.

Enraged at the interruption, Shears looked at Cortina, addressed him as a "goddamn greaser," and then turned to the old man and struck him on the side of his head with the barrel of his revolver. This action generated what many would later refer to as a twenty-year border war "that would exact its toll in lives and property on both sides of the river."

Angered at the injustice of Shears's actions, Cortina yanked his Colt revolver from his holster and fired a bullet into the marshal's shoulder, sending the lawman to the ground screaming in pain. As Shears lay bleeding on the floor, Cortina, with the help of some *vaqueros* who were in the cafe, helped to lift the old Mexican onto his horse behind him. Cortina transported the old man to his *rancho* where he nursed him back to health.

Cortina expected Shears, accompanied by a well-armed posse, to come after him, but for two months there was no reaction or response to the shooting. Cortina assumed the marshal was formulating plans for revenge, and so wisely avoided the town of Brownsville.

Cortina made plans to attend a fiesta across the Rio Grande in Matamoros on the evening of September 28. In addition to him and his cowhands, the event was attended by most of the Mexican residents from both sides of the river. Undoubtedly, the story of Marshal Shears's abuse of the elderly Mexican was told and retold. Long simmering hurts and hatreds at the way they had been treated by the Anglos burst forth and the air became heated with the telling.

Around 3:00 a.m. the following morning, Cortina led sixty armed and inebriated Mexicans across the river for a night raid and into the town of Brownsville. A large percentage of the town's population was still in Matamoros participating in the festivities. Cortina's contingent of men rode through the streets firing their weapons and shouting, "*Viva Mexico! Viva Cortina! Mueran los gringos!*" Kill the gringos!

Cortina decided it was time to deal with Glavecke and Shears, and he and his gang set out to find the two men. When they had no luck, they went to the jail, stormed it, and ordered jailer Robert Johnson to release all of the prisoners. When Johnson refused, they shot him. Wounded, the jailer fled and sought refuge in the nearby home of Viviano Garcia. Cortina's mob followed Johnson, and when Garcia stepped out onto his porch to order the intruders away, he was shot and killed. Stepping over his body, the raiders entered the home and killed Johnson.

The names Bill Noel and George Morris were advanced and the crowd grew even angrier. Noel and Morris were both known to have murdered several Mexicans over the years, but were never arrested or charged. The two men were searched for, located, and dispatched. By dawn, Cortina and his men had taken over the entire town of Brownsville.

Throughout this part of Texas, telegraph wires were fairly vibrating with the news of Cortina's night raid on Brownsville that, according to the reports, included looting, killing, and raping.

Cortina had decided to burn down the houses of a number of gringos he deemed particularly offensive. To accomplish this, he rode to the docks along the river to search for turpentine. As he looked through the supplies stacked there, he glanced up and spotted a troop of Mexican cavalry crossing the river. The force was led by General José María Jesús Carvajal, who was assisted by his commander of cavalry Don Miguel Tijerina. Tijerina also happened to be Cheno Cortina's cousin. Following a conversation with Carvajal and Tijerina, Cortina agreed to order his men out of Brownsville and gather at the military garrison in Matamoros for a conference. In a somewhat odd and ironic manner, the Mexican army saved Brownsville from complete destruction by Cheno Cortina's band of raiders.

Cortina remained in Matamoros for two days. When he finally returned to his rancho, he delivered the first of what would be several declarations. He was extremely critical of lawyers who swindled poor Mexicans out of their land, and in a strong statement said he would search the streets of Brownsville for such men and that, "Our personal enemies shall not possess our lands until they have fatted it with their own gore."

Cortina's pronouncement spread quickly throughout South Texas, and he soon found himself approached by dozens of volunteers. The working class Mexicans along the Rio Grande regarded him as a leader and a liberator, a man who could and would speak to and for their causes. Emotions ran high, and soon there was aggressive talk of driving the hated gringo oppressors from the area and returning much of South Texas to Mexico.

Brownsville mayor Stephen Powers heard all of the threats and harsh rhetoric. In addition, he was hearing the fears expressed by the frightened citizens. He set about organizing an appropriate defense of the town should it be attacked again. Powers sent requests for assistance to General David Twiggs, who commanded the US Army garrison in San Antonio, as well as Governor Hardin R. Runnels in Austin and President James Buchanan in Washington. So desperate was Powers that he sent another request to General Carvajal in Matamoros to provide a detachment of troops. Since the Mexican government was also interested in maintaining peace along the border between the two countries, they sent Carvajal, who arrived with a force and was immediately provided quarters at Fort Brown. Once ensconced in the fort, the general raised the Mexican flag over the compound. In spite of the added protection, Brownsville citizens continued to tremble in fear of another attack by Cortina and his raiders.

When Cortina had need of what a city had to offer, he avoided Brownsville and traveled across the river to Matamoros. Here, he was regarded as a hero. When he was on his own rancho, Mexicans would arrive from both sides of the border to gather around him and listen to speeches. All the while, however, Cortina maintained a low profile and was rarely seen by Brownsvillians and area Anglo ranchers.

Meanwhile, Mayor Powers and a man named W. B. Thompson organized a town guard of twenty-five men. They were called the Brownsville Tigers. Their role was to protect, and their orders were to patrol the town night and day. One afternoon while riding through a stand of dense brush outside of the town, several of the Tigers encountered sixty-five-year-old Tomás Cabrera. Cabrera was a known lieutenant in Cortina's small army, and was immediately arrested.

When Cortina learned of Cabrera's incarceration, he sent word to Powers that if the old man were not released he would attack the town. Powers refused to let Cabrera go, yet Cortina decided not to attack. Ascribing Cortina's refusal to attack to weakness, the emboldened Tigers decided to launch a strike on Cortina's ranch. They were joined by another forty men along with a contingent of militia from Matamoros led by Colonel Loranco. Oddly, this company consisted almost entirely of officers. The small army, transporting two small cannons, set out for the ranch on October 22, 1859.

The assembled force was apparently in no great hurry to encounter Cortina, for the march from just outside Brownsville to a point near Cortina's ranch, a total of just over six miles, took seven days. On arriving near the periphery of the ranch, the force encountered a number of Cortina's cowhands. Fearing that the vaqueros were armed and waiting in ambush, the Tigers and the Mexican army called for a halt. Discussion ensued with no clear strategy being determined. At one point, one of the members of the Tigers mounted his horse and suggested they all charge the ranch. No one would follow him.

A short time later, shots were fired. It remains unclear to this day which side fired first. At the outbreak of the fusillade, the Tigers and all of their reinforcements spurred their horses and drove their wagons back to Brownsville as fast as they could go. One of the men who traveled the seven days to reach Cortina's ranch said he made it back to his home in less than one hour. A few days after returning to Brownsville, the Tigers disbanded.

After the armies had fled, Cortina went to the site of the abbreviated skirmish and confiscated the two cannons that had been abandoned. Each morning thereafter, he would rise at dawn and fire a volley from the cannons to awaken the town of Brownsville.

Cortina appeared to enjoy the hostile relationship between himself and the townspeople. He would regularly intercept the mail carrier, have one of his literate cowhands open the mail and read it to him, and then have it resealed and sent on its way. On another occasion, Cortina rustled a small herd of cattle belonging to Sheriff James Browne. After keeping them for a time, he had them returned to the lawman along with an IOU for several he had butchered for meat. While the residents of Brownsville regarded themselves under siege by Cortina, the truth is that months passed without a single citizen being shot or even approached. But things were about to change.

Before much more time passed, Captain W. G. Tobin and his company of Texas Rangers arrived at Brownsville in response to desperate calls for help. Tobin's Rangers were described as "a sorry lot of riffraff recruited along the way from San Antonio." Tobin had not been in Brownsville for more than a few hours when he and his Rangers went to the jail and hung the sixty-five-year-old Tomás Cabrera, a completely unnecessary act. When Cortina heard of this cowardly deed, he and his men ambushed a party of the Rangers and killed three of them.

Tobin believed the solution to his problem was to reorganize the Brownsville Tigers. On November 24, 1859, this latest generation of the Tigers was led by Miflin Kenedy, who somehow acquired a twenty-four-pound howitzer. Newly emboldened, Tobin and Kenedy led the Rangers and Tigers once again to the edge of the Cortina holdings. This group of

Mifflin Kenedy

enforcers turned out to be no better than the previous save for the fact that as they fled after the first sounds of gunfire, they managed to take the howitzer with them.

In response to this most recent defeat, Cheno Cortina raised the flag of the Republic of Mexico over his rancho. He was regarded as a hero among the Mexicans as well as many Anglos far and wide for having routed the hated gringos twice. When he traveled across the river to

Matamoros, he and his contingent of vaqueros were greeted with cheers and even bugle calls and music. Cortina gained the reputation of a man who championed the downtrodden against the overwhelming numbers of swindling Yankees who were seen as persecutors of the Mexicans. There were calls for Cortina to form an army to chase the northerners out of the area.

Leading an army was not in the cards for Cortina. He did not believe this was the answer to the many problems facing the border residents. Instead, he issued more proclamations and called for greater protection of the rights of both Mexican landowners and workers. He was not interested in claiming tracts of Texas for Mexico; he simply wanted everyone who lived in his beloved country to get along with one another and work for common causes. It was not to be. While Cortina did not want war and conflict, his opposition did, and they brought it to him.

Things came to a head on November 12. According to a telegram sent by General Twiggs to Washington, Cortina's army, which allegedly grew to eight hundred men, had burned Brownsville to the ground and more than one hundred American citizens had been killed. A Major S. B. Heintzleman was ordered to lead seven companies of foot soldiers and two more of cavalry to take the field against Cortina.

Heintzleman reached Brownsville on December 5, 1859. Here, he was hesitantly joined by Tobin's cowardly Rangers. Together, the massed forces marched on the Cortinista army, eventually engaging it at El Ebonal near Brownsville. At the first encounter, Cortina lost eight men and ordered a retreat. Two of Tobin's Texas Rangers were killed, as was one Army trooper.

While Heintzleman was in pursuit of Cortina, Texas's Governor Runnels met with Texas Ranger captain John S. "Rip" Ford and begged him to go to Brownsville to assist the Army in saving Texas from the Mexican revolutionaries. Ford gathered fifty-three battle-tested Rangers armed only with handguns and a few rifles and provisions strapped to the back of their ponies, and headed for the border city. As they approached the town, they could hear the gunfire coming from El Ebonal. Ford

John S. "Rip" Ford, Texas Ranger

immediately led his men to Heintzleman's position and joined the Army in chasing the now retreating Cortinistas.

Cortina conducted his men along a route that paralleled the Rio Grande as they fled westward. Along the way, he lost control of his men. Their emotions now at a fever pitch as a result of the fighting, several of them left the column to raid, loot, and burn nearby ranches and settlements. By the end of December, the raiders had arrived at Rio

Grande City, one hundred miles upriver from Brownsville. Here, Cortina decided to make a stand and confront the oncoming US Army and Ford's Texas Rangers.

Ignoring Heintzleman's claims of command jurisdiction, Ford led his Rangers away from the soldiers and charged the Cortinista front line that consisted of three hundred fighters. Riding into the midst of the fighting vaqueros, the Rangers' superior marksmanship with the handguns proved immensely effective. In spite of being outnumbered six to one, the Rangers killed sixty of the Mexicans and sent the remainder into a confused and uncoordinated retreat. Not a single Ranger was killed.

Heintzleman's army closed in behind the Rangers and assisted in the pursuit, occasionally involving some of the fleeing Mexicans in skirmishes. Cortina, realizing he was outnumbered and out-armed, finally led his followers across the Rio Grande and into the safety of Mexico. As far as anyone knows, Cheno Cortina, the Red Robber of the Rio Grande, never returned to his ranch or to Texas. He had been badly beaten, and his revolution was over.

Cheno Cortina took up residence in the Mexican states of Nuevo Leon and Tamaulipas. It was rumored he tried his hand at cattle ranching again, but it is more likely that he pursued a life of rustling cattle and horses. It has been recorded that he served as a soldier for a time, and even dabbled in area politics. Though still revered and respected by his countrymen, Cortina soon became just another hard working *peon* eking out a living in a poor land.

To this day, ballads are sung about Cheno Cortina and his efforts to bring justice to the people and the country he loved so much.

CHAPTER TWO

The Salt War

ONE DAY IN 1872, A MAN ARRIVED IN EL PASO, TEXAS, FROM MISSOURI who was destined to play a major role in a historic conflict that was to forever alter ethnic relationships along the US–Mexico border. The man was Charles W. Howard, described as "a bulldog of a man with a barrel body, a menacing, heavy-featured face, and a carriage which testified that he had been a soldier." In time he came to be known as a fluent and refined speaker and a deadly marksman.

Howard was regarded as dangerous to many. He was a staunch and vocal Democrat in an environment dominated by Republicans. In a bold move, he decided to launch a political career in the opposition's stronghold. He preached the Democratic philosophy much as a rabid evangelist preached the gospel. In the process, he won few friends.

El Paso at this time was a predominantly Mexican community, with Anglos amounting to only 25 percent of the population. Here, however, Howard saw business opportunities, and he bided his time.

Downriver from El Paso was the tiny village of Ysleta, the oldest settlement in Texas and founded by priests and Indians fleeing from the Pueblo revolt in New Mexico in 1680. Twenty miles downriver to the southeast was San Elizario, a Mexican community and one that was to serve as the setting for the final chapter in Howard's life, and death.

Life along the border in this upriver part of Texas proceeded much as it had for hundreds of years. To the Mexicans, the international boundary represented by the Rio Grande was paid scant attention, if any at all. They passed back and forth across the river often on a variety of errands and missions and to conduct business. Families on both sides were related to one another; farmers and ranchers on the Mexican side grazed their cattle, horses, and goats on the pastures found on the American side. The notion of a boundary established by a bunch of newcomer gringos made little sense to them.

To Charles Howard's discredit, he was never able to accommodate the cultural differences between the Mexicans and whites, particularly the Mexican attitude toward written codes of law and private property. The Mexicans were firm believers in the notion that power and decisions originate with the people, not with law books.

Mexican notions of operating along the border clashed with Howard's ideals, and the differences in philosophies and practices gradually reached a boiling point. Added to this volatile mix was greed. And it all had to do with one of the most common minerals—salt.

One of the greatest salt deposits in the Southwest lay near the western foothills of the majestic Guadalupe Mountains of Texas. The deposits were a remnant of a shallow prehistoric sea, and occasional rains turned them into a chain of lakes that stretched north-south for twenty-five miles. Mexicans from both sides of the Rio Grande knew of these salt lakes, but chose to travel to a location in the Tularosa Basin seventy miles north of El Paso to harvest the mineral.

In 1862, the Mexican salt harvesters decided to open up the beds near the Guadalupe Mountains. Private ownership had closed off the Tularosa supply, and the quality of salt to the east was deemed higher. In time, a road from Fort Quitman, located on the banks of the Rio Grande below San Elizario, was laid out. Though it was a rugged two-day trip to the salt lakes and the threat of attack by Apache Indians was constant, the traffic was high as dozens arrived from as far away as one hundred miles south of the river to harvest the salt. Men whose farms or businesses failed knew they could turn to mining the salt to make a living.

The notion that someone could take their salt deposits away from them never entered the minds of the Mexicans. As soon as the Fort Quitman road was opened up, however, El Paso politicians caught the scent of profits to be made from the salt. While an El Paso cartel was making plans to legally acquire the salt beds, they were thwarted by rancher Samuel A. Maverick. Maverick acquired enough funding to purchase two sections of the prime deposits.

Initially, the Mexican salt harvesters were upset and disappointed with this development, but they soon learned that a number of good salt deposits lay outside of Maverick's claim. Noticing the continuation of the profitable salt harvesting, the El Paso politicians resumed their plans to profit from it. The initial group that directed their intentions toward the salt beds included W. W. Mills, Albert Jennings Fountain, Gaylord Clarke, A. H. French, B. F. Williams, and J. M. Luján. They were soon referred to as the "Salt Ring."

In 1868, Fountain and Mills found reasons not to get along. Fountain dropped out of the group and undertook to lead an "Anti-Salt Ring" faction. As Mills and Fountain continued to snipe at one another, Charles Howard arrived in town.

W. W. Mills had fought for the Union and was a powerful Republican leader in this part of Texas. He had been named collector of customs and was regarded as a political boss of the region. Aligned with Mills was Louis Cardis. An Italian, Cardis had lived in El Paso since 1864, spoke excellent Spanish, and was highly regarded by the Mexican population, who referred to him as Don Luis.

The Salt Ring sought and welcomed the influence of another man— Father Antonio Borrajo, the San Elizario parish priest. Borrajo, more than anyone else, held great power over the Mexicans on both sides of the river. Borrajo was strong-willed, had a volcanic temperament, and disliked women and anyone who crossed him. Though Borrajo courted members of the Salt Ring, he disliked Americans in general, regarding them as invaders to this land. On arriving in Borrajo's church territory, they had established secular schools and enacted laws preventing Mexican citizens from burying their dead in consecrated ground behind the church—for sanitary reasons, they explained.

Col. Albert Jennings Fountain

Mills and Fountain remained at one another's throats, attacking each other in print as the occasion demanded. Mills had Fountain indicted in US District Court on eighteen different counts, all of which he was acquitted. Mills supported the candidacy of his father-in-law for governor; Fountain backed his opponent, who won. Fountain was then elected to a State Senate seat which further infuriated Mills. Mills was subsequently removed from his position as collector of customs and blamed Fountain.

Louis Cardis

A short time after being elected to the Texas State Senate, Fountain was paid a visit by Father Borrajo, who inquired as to his intentions regarding the salt lakes. Fountain explained he would try to acquire them for the citizens of the El Paso district and introduced legislation to that effect. Borrajo said he had a better idea. He suggested that Fountain, using his influence and his potential for acquiring funding, purchase the lakes for himself and charge a reasonable price for the salt. Borrajo said he would instruct his people to pay the price, and then he and Fountain could split the profits. Fountain's refusal sent the priest into a rage. He cursed and threatened the senator before departing.

Mills's friend Cardis did not want Fountain's plan to become a reality, as it would defeat the purposes of the Salt Ring. Cardis aligned himself with Borrajo. Borrajo and Cardis lobbied intensively with Rio Grande Valley residents, persuading them that Fountain's plan was another political move to keep the Mexicans from getting the salt. Though Fountain worked hard for what he thought was the honest and appropriate way to deal with the salt issue, it soon became clear to him that the residents wanted no part of it. Fountain withdrew his bill. The situation was soon to grow worse.

On December 7, 1870, Salt Ring member B. F. Williams had too much to drink at Ben Dowell's Saloon in El Paso. Williams, who despised Fountain, began cursing the aims and philosophies of the senator as well as Judge Gaylord Clarke. Though Clarke was a member of the Salt Ring, he remained a good friend to Fountain. Into this blistering stream of threats and curses stepped Fountain himself. As he passed through the door of the saloon, Williams pulled and fired his two-shot Derringer, sending both bullets into Fountain. The senator, wounded, attacked Williams with his cane. Williams turned and fled to his nearby room and barricaded the door. Fountain limped to his own house to retrieve his rifle. Along the way he ran into Judge Clarke who, in turn, ordered Captain French of the state police to arrest Williams.

After arriving at Williams's room, Clarke and French attempted to break down the door. During a pause in their efforts, Williams stepped out with a double-barrel shotgun and emptied both charges into Clarke's breast from only a foot or two away. As Clarke fell to the ground, Fountain was approaching the scene. He fired his rifle at Williams at the same time French fired his pistol. Both bullets stuck Williams and he fell to the ground, dead.

This incident caused Fountain to rethink his situation and rearrange his priorities. For months, he had known his life was in danger, and he was having few successes in attempting to serve the people of his district. When his term in the legislature ended in 1874, he packed up his family and moved to Mesilla, New Mexico, where it was not long before he established himself as a talented and tenacious legislator, newspaper editor, and Indian fighter.

Charles Howard observed all of these goings-on from a distance. The killing of Williams appeared to generate a bit of a recess in the violence and enmity surrounding the salt deposits. The economic panic of 1873 forced many El Paso businesses to close. Area residents were more concerned about making a living than about the Salt Ring. Many moved away.

Author C. L. Sonnichsen advanced the notion that the feud between the salt and anti-salt factions would have likely died away except for the presence of Howard, whom he referred to as "the center of a whirlwind of violence that dwarfed that which had gone before."

Howard has been described as "pugnacious" and "assertive." He found something in the local politics that appealed to him, and he soon entered the arena to take on A. J. Fountain. When it was learned that Howard would oppose Fountain, Cardis and Borrajo aligned themselves with him. At first, Howard and Cardis worked well together. Cardis liked to work behind the scenes; Howard loved to orate. Cardis was able to mobilize the Mexican population. Howard found success in bullying the Americans.

Howard ran for district attorney against J. P. Hague, a Fountain man, and won by a vote of 477 to 120. In 1874, Howard worked to get Cardis elected to the State Legislature, with Father Borrajo running interference. Borrajo visited all of his parishioners and told them that if they did not vote for Cardis they would not be buried in consecrated ground. Cardis won by a landslide.

Howard was soon appointed district judge and was now the supreme judicial authority over a huge geographic region. Things were going well for the Howard-Cardis-Borrajo faction. Howard decided to get married to Louisa Zimpleman of Manor, Texas, the daughter of a well-known businessman and banker. In the summer of 1877, Louisa died following a protracted illness, but Howard and Louisa's father remained close friends and business partners.

It is not clear what Louisa's death had to do with a change in Howard, but within days of her funeral he became more arrogant and bullying than he had been. He harbored a growing scorn for any and all who opposed his will and wishes. It was not long before he and Cardis began to collide, and it was the issue of salt that set them at odds.

Cardis and Borrajo attempted to get Howard to agree to a scheme to claim the salt beds near the Guadalupe Mountains. In response, Howard manifested rage at the two men for their suggestion, and later told Fountain that he had separated himself from Cardis and Borrajo because they were trying to force him into "some monstrous schemes."

The disagreements grew hostile and bitter, and Howard and Cardis soon despised each other with fiery intensity. Howard called Cardis "a liar, a coward, a mischief maker, a meddler; such a thing as could only spring from the decaying carcass of an effete people."

Delegates to the Constitutional Convention had been elected in June 1875, and both Howard and Cardis were candidates. Howard beat Cardis at both the precinct and district conventions. Cardis loudly announced that Howard's victory was accomplished by fraud and trickery. Cardis ran as an Independent in the August election and beat Howard soundly.

Things became even more bitter. An irrigation project slated for San Elizario to be funded by district money was slow in getting underway. Cardis told the Mexicans living for hundreds of miles along the Rio Grande that it was Howard's fault. When Howard arrived in Presidio to attend District Court there, citizens mobbed him. At the next election, Howard was out as district judge, but Cardis had been re-elected to the State Legislature. On two occasions—one in Austin and another in San Antonio—Howard delivered a public beating to Cardis.

Using the name of his father-in-law Zimpleman, Howard filed and took over the claim of the salt lakes staked out ten years earlier by Samuel Maverick. He also filed on additional salt deposits in the area. This act was disturbing to the Mexican population, for the salt was often the only thing standing between them and starvation. The population was desperate. There had been no rainfall for some time, the river was almost dry, and corn and other crops were almost non-existent. Now, their opportunities to make a little money from the salt had been taken away from them. Resentment of the Americans, particularly Howard, was rising. They were convinced that the politician had deceived them.

When Father Borrajo learned of Howard's attempt to control the salt lakes, he went into a rage. Borrajo despised all Americans, in particular Howard. Borrajo also reserved a large helping of hate for Charles Ellis. Ellis owned a store and mill on the northwest limit of San Elizario and had married one of the Mexican citizens. Ellis had also served as sheriff and tax collector from 1871 to 1873. Ellis was a supporter of Howard, and that was sufficient to draw ire from Borrajo.

Early in 1877, Father Borrajo received an assignment from the church to move to a parish in Mexico. Because the priest relished his power and control over the citizens in San Elizario, he informed all who would listen that he was not leaving. Bishop Salpointe of the Diocese of Tucson set out for San Elizario to discuss the matter with the recalcitrant priest. Salpointe's carriage was stopped on the road several miles from the town by Borrajo and his followers. The bishop was insulted and threatened with serious trouble should he proceed on to the town.

Bishop Salpointe finally made his way to San Elizario, but Borrajo saw to it that no one would provide him with a room; he was forced to set up a camp on the outskirts. In the morning, he returned to El Paso. Borrajo rejoiced in his victory, but it was to be a short celebration. The Bishop of Durango (Mexico) transferred him to Guadalupe Bravos, a smaller parish on the Mexican side of the river and ten miles downstream.

One morning, Charles Howard set off in his buggy to the salt lakes to oversee the completion of a new survey relative to his acquiring the property. He was accompanied by a surveyor, three black men, and three Mexicans. When the party reached San Elizario, the Mexicans dropped out, explaining that Luis Cardis instructed them not to continue. Shorthanded and angry, Howard set up camp near Fort Quitman.

Luis Cardis maintained a stage station near one end of the fort. When he spotted Howard and his surveyor nearby, he dashed inside his station hoping not to be seen. Howard, however, had noticed Cardis and went in after him. He found Cardis cowering under a table and didn't have the heart to shoot him. Cardis filed charges against Howard for assault.

When Howard finished with the survey, he posted notices around the Mexican communities stating that the salt lakes belonged to him and anyone who entered them would be prosecuted. This angered the populace, and the rift between Howard and the community grew wider. Cardis did his best to keep the citizens stirred up, then left for El Paso because he did not want to remain in town if things turned violent. A mob composed of a number of the most aggressive citizens began to form and demanded an arrest warrant for Howard. When the justice of the peace explained that he could not do such a thing legally, the mob locked him in the jail. The next day, the mob also locked the county judge in the jail for refusing to issue a warrant.

In the meantime, Howard was fuming, and stated to his servant that he was going to kill Cardis. He returned to Ysleta and spent the night at the home of the sheriff there. In the morning, he awoke to find the house surrounded. Squaring his shoulders, Howard stepped outside to face the mob. Leaders Chico Barela and Leon Granillo told Howard that he was their prisoner, and they seized him. He was dragged through the streets of Ysleta in the company of forty armed men. This party was joined by thirty more. Howard was placed on a horse and taken to San Elizario.

On arriving, Howard was led to a house and placed under guard. Before being locked in a small room, Howard stated later that he "found from 200 to 250 more Mexicans under arms" and that they appeared "sullen, ferocious." Howard was kept in the room for three days and three nights and was permitted visits from no one. He was certain he would be killed, so late on the third day he consented to make any agreements required of him. Father Bourgade, the new priest assigned to San Elizario, handled the negotiation. Howard also agreed not to persecute anyone for his abduction and imprisonment.

With this, the mob sent a messenger to Cardis asking for advice. Cardis, who had been advised by the sheriff that he could be in trouble should Howard come to any harm, sent word that no blood should be shed, and then he assisted in drawing up the papers to be signed by Howard. Howard agreed to let the courts decide who owned the salt lakes, leave the area within twenty-four hours and never return, provide bond for his future conduct, and drop charges against the men who challenged his ownership of the lakes. After signing, he was allowed to go free.

Howard fled to Mesilla, New Mexico, where A. J. Fountain provided him sanctuary. Once there, Howard telegraphed the governor of Texas to warn him of the potential danger of an invasion from Mexico. He was also successful in panicking Sheriff Kerber to try to get troops brought in from Fort Craig. District Judge Allen Blacker, caught up in the frenzy, messaged the governor telling him that in his part of Texas the civil authorities were powerless and that life and property were threatened. The governor tried to mobilize the Texas Rangers, but the nearest detachment was five hundred miles from San Elizario. Even Cardis telegraphed the governor, explained that things in the area had quieted down somewhat and that, "It is mainly through my efforts that peace has been established. . . ."

In Mesilla, Howard seethed with rage. Though he felt he could not be held to the agreement he signed since it was done under duress, he remained humiliated, a humiliation he attributed to Cardis. All of his thoughts were on revenge, and the opportunity was not long in coming.

On October 7, G. H. Wahl, the Ysleta County clerk, visited Cardis and warned him of the danger of encountering Howard. Cardis showed Wahl two pistols he carried and assured him he was ready for any trouble. Cardis was well aware of Howard's threats on his life. On that same day, Howard had driven to El Paso from Mesilla. He rode with a company of soldiers from Fort Bayard that had been ordered to San Elizario by Colonel Hatch. Following lunch on October 10, Howard rose from the table, picked up his shotgun, and told his servant that he "must have my revenge." With that, he strode out the door.

A short time later, Howard entered Solomon Schultz's store. After his eyes adjusted to the dim light, he spotted Cardis dictating a letter to the store's bookkeeper, Adolph Krakauer, his back to Howard. Storekeeper Schultz, perceiving the potential for trouble, greeted Howard loud enough so that Cardis could hear. Cardis jumped from his chair and stepped behind a tall bookkeeper's desk, the closest thing to protection in the store. Schultz called for Krakauer to get away from the two men and then pleaded with Howard not to shoot.

Howard fired one of the charges of buckshot under the desk, the pellets striking Cardis in the stomach. As the victim staggered out from behind the useless barricade, Howard fired the remaining charge into his left breast. With Cardis dead, Howard turned and left the building. He immediately returned to Mesilla.

Accounts of the shooting provided by those present implied that Cardis made no attempt to defend himself. Howard, however, claimed Cardis held a pistol in his right hand and that he raised it preparatory to firing when he, Howard, defended himself with the shotgun.

Ysleta's Sheriff Kerber was quoted as saying that killing Cardis was a good thing and suggested that a monument should be erected to Howard "for delivering us from a tyrannical and unscrupulous scoundrel."

The Mexican communities up and down the river felt differently; resentment was high, feverish, and soon the perception was that the life of every white American in the region was endangered. Kerber attempted to deputize a number of men in the event that violence ensued, but few desired the job. A telegram was sent forthwith to Colonel Hatch requesting immediate help.

From Ysleta downriver to San Elizario, nerves were frayed and ragged, the citizens long tired of the heavy-handed dominance by white businessmen, politicians, and lawmakers. Men from Mexico crossed the river in twos and threes, groups of a half dozen or more, all of them armed, all of them coming to the aid of their kinsmen. On the Mexican side of the river, Father Borrajo continued to denounce the wicked Yankees and their persecution of the lowly.

Major John B. Jones of the Texas Rangers was ordered to El Paso to determine what was going on and implement a strategy to forestall any violence. He arrived in Mesilla alone and met with Fountain and Howard. Following this, he traveled to El Paso where he found the citizenry in a state of fear and nervousness. The San Elizario mob, amid threats, had served notice on Howard's bondsmen to pay up. Jones and Sheriff Kerber received a message from a group of men including Ellis, Atkinson, and others asking for help. They had taken refuge inside a house in San Elizario and were afraid to go out.

Jones decided he must do something. He traveled to San Elizario and asked to meet with the leaders. He told them if their rights to the salt lakes had been violated the courts would take care of the matter. The assembly ignored Jones and the matter of the salt lakes. They told him that Howard had violated the agreement and they wanted to call in the bond. Jones promised that Howard would have to account for his behavior and the group agreed to adhere to Jones's advice and recommendations.

Just when he was receiving some positive reactions from the citizens, Jones made a terrible mistake. He told them that he intended to send a company of Texas Rangers into town to maintain order. The citizens told him they would raise their own company and elect their own officers to maintain order. Jones refused to agree to any of their proposal. The next morning, Jones returned to El Paso, leaving behind a populace that was angrier than when he arrived.

When Jones got to El Paso, he set about trying to recruit a company of Rangers. He telegraphed the adjutant general requesting a second lieutenant's commission for John B. Tays, who he wanted to head a detachment. Jones then undertook the task of recruiting men to serve as Rangers in the command. Like Kerber, Jones had an equally difficult time in assembling a satisfactory group of men. Volunteers were few, and Jones set about pulling in men, as author Sonnichsen writes, "out of holes and corners." Not a single one of the twenty recruits would have qualified as a Texas Ranger under normal circumstances, a standard that was already low.

Tays took command of this rag-tag bunch of loafers. As soon as he acquired arms, ammunition, and horses, he led the detachment to their new quarters at San Elizario.

Charles Howard traveled from Mesilla to El Paso to appear before Justice of the Peace Guadalupe Carbajal where he was arraigned for the murder of Cardis. He was admitted to bail in the amount of four thousand dollars. Howard was advised to stay away from the valley until court met.

The arrogant and cocky Howard, however, did not stay away. With a number of people who agreed to testify on his behalf, he was confident that he would be found innocent of the murder of Cardis. He remained in El Paso, walking the streets and stopping in the bars to chat with old friends and new.

Major Jones was aware that Howard refused the advice to lay low, but for some reason was convinced that he was safe. Jones returned to Austin. He had no sooner arrived when he received a letter from Hays who informed him that Howard, on traveling the road from Mesilla to El Paso, shot the dog of a rancher. Armed men rushed at Howard and threatened him, but Howard paid them one hundred dollars and rode away.

John McBride was Howard's agent in San Elizario. On December 2, McBride rode up to the El Paso Customs House and hurried up to Inspector Joseph Magoffin and Collector S. C. Slade and informed them that a caravan of sixteen carts and sixty yoke of oxen was on its way to the salt lakes. Among the party were a significant number of Mexican nationals. Magoffin enlisted an escort of a half-dozen soldiers, heaved his heavy frame into a buggy, and struck out for San Elizario. On reaching the town, he questioned a number of the citizens and learned that dozens of men from both sides of the river made up the party traveling to the salt lakes. Even the *alcalde* of Guadalupe, the town across the river from San Elizario, was a member of the party.

Magoffin met with citizen Cirpiano Alderete, who informed him that the community cared little about what the Anglos thought and did and that they were going to even the score. Magoffin hurried on to Quitman where he noted that several carts had come up from Mexico to join the caravan. He followed the well-marked trail and just past sundown arrived at their camp. When the customs inspector approached, a half-dozen Mexicans leveled rifles at him. He informed them that they would have to return with him the following morning. When he approached the camp the next morning, he found they were gone. He learned later that the Mexicans had intended to kill him.

Learning of the raid in the salt lakes, Howard initiated legal proceedings. On December 12, he obtained a writ to secure eight hundred bushels of salt taken from his claim "forcibly and with violence." When the citizens of San Elizario and other communities along the river learned of this they grew even angrier. Father Bourgade wrote to Major Jones that the salt was vital to the economy of the area, and that three-fourths of the citizens were on the verge of starving because of a bad growing season. Harvesting the salt was the only way they would make a living.

Captain Thomas Blair arrived from Fort Bayard but was instructed not to interfere unless aliens were implicated. Blair informed Tays he would stand by to assist. The governor of Texas telegrammed San Elizario leaders reminding them it was necessary for them to obey the laws. The leaders were unimpressed.

Howard had an opportunity to withdraw his charges and allow the matter to return to some level of calm. Instead, he repeated his intention to prosecute if they took his salt. On December 12, the brazen Howard traveled to San Elizario to make certain the residents understood his position. He was escorted by a small Ranger force.

Somehow the residents knew Howard was coming. Father Bourgade telegraphed Lieutenant Tays that the town was quite agitated and most of the men were armed in anticipation of trouble. Concerned for the safety of Howard, Bourgade rode toward Ysleta to meet Howard. He came upon a large band of armed and angry Mexicans, several of whom lived across the river. The leader of the group was Chico Barela. Barela had been particularly close to Cardis.

Tays caught up with Howard at Ysleta and warned him of the dire consequences of his continuing. He informed Howard he had sent for Captain Blair. Howard was adamant and continued on to San Elizario, eventually arriving at Ranger headquarters. Howard took up residence in a nearby house.

Around this time, Blair, who had received Tays's message, left Ysleta with fourteen men. By 9:00 p.m. he had arrived on the outskirts of San Elizario where he encountered a number of armed Mexicans, but they were allowed to pass. As they reached the edge of town, their forward movement was blocked by a number of armed men who forbade them to continue. Blair insisted on meeting with their leader, and thirty minutes later Chico Barela appeared.

Barela informed Blair he could not enter the town and that they were going to "take Howard, and nothing can stop us." He told Blair that if he and his men tried to interfere they would meet resistance. Blair wanted to argue the point but Barela was insistent, informing the soldier that this matter "is none of your business." Blair led his force back to Ysleta.

In the morning Blair telegraphed his commanding officer that the trouble in San Elizario had been greatly exaggerated. Texas's Governor Hubbard nevertheless wired President Hayes requesting aid in repelling an invasion. His request was responded to positively, but things move slowly in the federal government.

Howard visited Ellis's store where he found a dozen men, all armed, and keeping a watch on the town from the windows. Late in the evening, Ellis stepped out the front door of his building, and then returned to inform Howard that he was concerned about the mood of the townspeople. Down the street, Chico Barela was addressing a large crowd, telling them how he had run off Captain Blair and his soldiers. Barela told the crowd they would deal with Howard in the morning.

Ellis was spotted eavesdropping on the goings-on and was seized. With several of the citizens chanting, "Now is the time!" they tossed a rope around Ellis and proceeded to drag him up and down the gravel street. After the third pass, Ellis was begging for his life, when one of the horsemen, Manuel Lopez, told several onlookers to stab Ellis to death. One of them did.

Howard, his servant Wesley Owens, Deputy Sheriff Andrew Loomis of Pecos County, and twenty Rangers remained secluded in the Ranger quarters. Tays estimated they had enough food and water to sustain them in the event of a siege. The following morning, Tays looked out the window and saw hundreds of armed men formed in picket lines around the building. As he stared, a shot was fired and a bullet shattered the window. Howard approached Tays and said that everyone would be better off if he simply surrendered to the townspeople, that he would not permit others to be killed because of him.

A short time later, one of Barela's lieutenants called out to the Rangers to turn Howard over to them. If they refused, said the spokesman, they would take him by force and then kill him as well as anyone who tried to defend him. By now, several of the Rangers were grumbling about the possibility of losing their lives over this man Howard.

Around mid-morning a shot was fired that killed one of the Rangers. Sporadic shooting took place throughout most of the rest of the day. After sundown, one of the Rangers climbed up on the roof and waved a white flag of surrender. He was immediately fired upon and forced back into the building.

On the evening of the second day of the siege, a wave of townspeople charged the Ellis store. The assault resulted in the killing of another man. As those inside piled sacks of flour in the store windows for protection, gunfire continued throughout the night. For four days and nights, the Rangers and other occupants of the Ellis store held out against assaults and continued gunfire. Deputy Sheriff Loomis was determined to leave. Under a flag of truce, he was allowed to walk out of the building. As Loomis prepared to depart town, however, he was seized by a number of men and locked up in an adobe prison.

When Monday morning arrived, the sixth day of the siege, Tays looked out a window and saw that the Mexicans had dug rifle pits and erected breastworks in the front of the Ranger headquarters. Once again, the townspeople demanded that Howard be turned over to them. If he was not, they said they would blow up the building. Tays tried to stall for time. The Mexicans then told Tays that if he gave up Howard, and if Howard gave up all claims to the salt lakes, then no harm would come to occupants of the building. Howard informed Tays that he would surrender to them. He added that, "They will kill me."

Tays tried to talk Howard out of surrendering, but to no avail. Tays escorted him to the home of Guillermo Gándara where he was delivered to Barela. Barela persuaded a man named Atkinson to turn over eleven thousand dollars, the approximate amount of Howard's bond. Barela then stated that if the Rangers surrendered and Howard consented to leave the area forever, all could go free. All agreed.

Barela then sent a message to Father Borrajo advising him that an agreement had been reached. According to one report, the priest replied, "Shoot all the gringos and I will absolve you."

Atkinson returned to the Ranger quarters and informed all assembled there of the arrangement that they could leave with their horses and guns. Atkinson told them Lieutenant Tays was waiting for them. When the Rangers arrived at the mob headquarters, however, they were disarmed, forced into a small room, and placed under guard. Tays, who was still conferring with Barela, was unaware that his men had been made prisoners. Tays informed Barela that he would not leave until Howard was allowed to go free. With that, Tays was lifted bodily and thrown into the room with his Rangers.

As the anger and resentment surged and the desire for revenge against those who had wronged them grew, Mexicans from both sides of the river congregated in San Elizario until there were more than five hundred surging through the streets of the tiny community calling for Charles Howard's execution. When the momentum and volume of the mob had reached its height, a group of a dozen men entered the house, seized Howard, and shoved him out the door. As he was escorted out into the street, the mob quieted, and all was silence as he was placed against a wall. Desiderio Apodaca recruited five riflemen to serve as executioners. Each one of them was a resident of Guadalupe Bravos on the other side of the Rio Grande.

Howard warned the assembled mass that if they killed him, hundreds more would die in payment for his death. The mob paid no heed to his statement and a moment later the order to fire was given. Howard fell to the ground, mortally wounded yet still alive, writhing in pain. Jesús Telles, a notorious horse thief who preyed on ranches on both sides of the river, dashed up to Howard who was contorting in agony. Telles unsheathed his machete, raised it over his head, and swung a mighty blow at the dying man's head. At the last second, Howard twisted away and Telles missed and severed two toes from his own foot. As Telles limped away, several others approached with their machetes and hacked away at the body until it no longer moved.

Next, Atkinson and McBride were brought outside to face the mob. When it was clear that they, too, were to be executed, Atkinson reminded Chico Barela that he had given his word that they would be released. Barela had little to say as the mob screamed for Atkinson's life. Demonstrating remarkable poise, Atkinson removed his coat, unbuttoned his shirt, and, facing his executioners, told them that when he gave the word to fire at his heart. At his command, five bullets pierced his torso, every one of them missing his heart. Still standing, he said. "Higher, you bastards!" Two more shots were fired, knocking Atkinson to the ground, but he was still alive. At this point, Jesús Garcia stepped up and shot him in the head.

McBride was brought forward. He said not a word and he was shot down by the firing squad. With McBride's death, the mob began screaming again for more blood and shouts of "Kill all the gringos." Barela addressed the crowd and said his men were committed to fight any further persecution but for now there would be no more killing. The bodies of Howard, Atkinson, and McBride were dragged away to the edge of town with ropes tied to saddle horns. There, they were stripped of their clothes, hacked to pieces, and their remains thrown into an abandoned well.

Then the looting began. A number of residents from Guadalupe Bravos came with carts in anticipation of such a thing. Both the house and store of Ellis had been stripped of furniture, dishes, clothes, and food. Author Sonnichsen wrote that thirty thousand dollars in money and goods was taken over the next two days.

The Texas Rangers, who were still secluded in their quarters, were ordered to exit the building without their arms. Their horses were returned to them, and they were told to return to Ysleta. Tays, still trying to maintain some semblance of control and authority, demanded the return of their weapons but Barela refused. Only too happy to get away from San Elizario, most of the rag-tag party of Texas Rangers scattered like rabbits.

When Tays returned to El Paso, he received an odd bit of news. He learned that Captain Blair had been readying a command of eighteen men to come to his aid, but had not planned on departing for another three months.

Sheriff Kerber had been ordered by Texas's Governor Hubbard to assemble a posse, but he was unable to enlist any men in El Paso. Desperate, he appealed to the citizenry in Silver City, 120 straight-line miles away, and was surprised and delighted when thirty men answered the call. Colonel Hatch arrived with a contingent of soldiers. When all were assembled, the party departed from El Paso to San Elizario prepared for an invasion. Accompanying the contingent was a wagon transporting four coffins for the bodies of the murdered Americans.

On the outskirts of Ysleta, the posse paused to search the home of Crescencio Irigoyen where they found a pistol and a rifle that had belonged to the Rangers. More guns and ammunition were located and confiscated at other locations. Irigoyen and an Indian named Santiago Durán were taken prisoner, bound hand and foot, and forced to ride atop the coffins. Before the force arrived at San Elizario, the two men were executed. In standard Texas Ranger fashion, Lieutenant Tays reported that the two prisoners were shot while trying to escape.

Passing through the town of Socorro, located between Ysleta and San Elizario, one of Kerber's men was shot in the foot by a sniper. Jesús Telles, minus two toes, was encountered in Socorro and cut down by gunfire from the posse. Another Socorro citizen, Cruz Cháves, was also gunned down. By this time, a scout reported to Kerber and Hatch that gunmen were waiting for the party on the road to San Elizario. The Rangers remained in Socorro for the night and were joined by reinforcements. The following morning they continued on to San Elizario. On arriving, they met no organized resistance whatsoever and were, for the most part, ignored.

The Texas Rangers and the Silver City volunteers returned to Ysleta where most of them remained until Christmas. While there, a number of them were involved in thefts from stores. During a fight, one of the Rangers shot and killed another. Two of them were charged with rape.

John B. Jones, Texas Ranger

Hearing of such goings-on, Captain Blair wrote to Kerber expressing his dismay and disappointment at this turn of events, stating that he had learned that some of the Ysleta citizenry were forced to flee across the river to Mexico to escape the predations and violence of the so-called lawmen. Lieutenant Tays sent his resignation to Austin where it was accepted with no delay. Tays is the only Texas Ranger in history who surrendered to an enemy.

An official investigation was undertaken by the US Congress. In the end reports were printed, read, discussed, and set aside. Not a single decision was ever made regarding anything related to the salt war. An El Paso County grand jury indicted Chico Barela and six others who were deeply involved for their stated crimes. Rewards were offered for their capture, but no one ever came forth to provide information or collect the money and the men were never arrested. For decades, San Elizario citizens remained bitter toward the intrusion of Anglos in the area, but passions eventually subsided.

J. C. Ford was named as agent for the Zimpleman salt claims. When this was made known, residents of towns on both sides of the river applied to him for permission to harvest salt and it was granted.

Known today as the El Paso Salt War, it ended, as author Sonnischen wrote, like most wars—"wasteful and unnecessary."

CHAPTER THREE

Incident at Indian Hot Springs

INDIAN HOT SPRINGS IS ON THE NORTH SIDE OF THE RIO GRANDE AND only a few yards from the river in southern Hudspeth County, Texas. The site was named for the seven warm to hot springs (81–117 degrees F) found in the immediate area and at the southern end of the Quitman Mountains. In addition to a few cottonwood and willow trees along the river, the area is replete with cactus, salt cedar, mesquite, and creosote bush. Animal life in the area includes white tail deer, mule deer, javelina, bobcat, mountain lion, quail, dove, and at least two species of rattle-snakes. Archaeological evidence indicates that the springs were used by Paleo-Indians as well as by more contemporary tribes such as Comanches and Apaches. The Indians believed the waters possessed curative powers.

Today, Indian Hot Springs and the surrounding area are sparsely populated. A few ranches struggle to raise cattle in the arid environment of the Chihuahuan Desert. US Border Patrol personnel far outnumber the resident population. As a result, the Indian Hot Springs setting remains relatively peaceful and serene, disturbed only occasionally by the hum of insects, the singing of birds, and the occasional bleat of a goat coming from the tiny Mexican community across the river—Ojo Caliente—or the bray of a burro that wandered across the shallow river to graze on a patch of enticing grasses. It is difficult to believe that in this location in 1880 a band of Apaches launched an attack on a contingent of US cavalry troops, killing seven of them. A tiny cemetery containing the graves of the slain soldiers can still be seen at Indian Hot Springs today.

A major and notorious chief of the Warm Springs band of Chiricahua Apaches was Victorio. In addition to Warm Springs Apaches, he also had among his large contingent of raiders members of the Mimbres and Mescalero bands. Victorio and his followers roamed and raided up and down the Rio Grande Valley from central New Mexico to the Texas border, attacking wagon trains, solitary travelers, small settlements, and even churches. The Indians took what horses and other livestock was available, as well as children who were used as slaves. When they departed, they left dead bodies in their wake.

Victorio and his people also had a number of confrontations with the US Army. Much to the dismay and disgust of the military leaders, Victorio either came out the victor in these skirmishes and battles, or simply vanished into the landscape. Rewards were offered for this warrior, but attempts to catch him invariably ended in failure.

In late August of 1878, the Apache chief undertook what has been termed Victorio's War. After escaping from the San Carlos Indian Reservation in southeastern Arizona, Victorio led guerrilla raids across the American Southwest and northern Mexico. When they had completed their depredations across this vast swath of landscape, they retreated into the Tres Castillos Mountains located about one hundred miles south-southeast of El Paso in the Mexican state of Chihuahua. Here they intended to rest men and horses for a time before returning to the United States to continue their pillaging.

Victorio's plans were doomed never to materialize. Weary of Apache raids in the area, the Mexican government sent an army under the leadership of General Joaquin Terrazas to locate and confront Victorio and his warriors, engage them in battle, and rid the countryside of this menace once and for all. On October 15, 1880, Terrazas's army surrounded Victorio's campsite in the Tres Castillo Mountains and attacked. All but seventeen of the Apaches were slain.

Some controversy exists regarding the death of Victorio. Terrazas claimed that the famous Apache chief was shot and killed by a scout employed by the Mexican army. Others, however, insisted that Victorio, rather than be captured by the Mexicans, took his own life. Meanwhile, the seventeen Apaches who escaped fled out of the mountains northeastward toward the Rio Grande intending to cross at Indian Hot Springs.

Fort Quitman was established on September 28, 1858. It was located south of the present-day town of Sierra Blanca. To the fort were assigned members of the Ninth and Tenth US Cavalry. The members of these cavalry units, with the exception of the officers, were black, and were known as Buffalo Soldiers. The Buffalo Soldiers had distinguished themselves in a number of armed conflicts with Indians throughout much of the Southwest and were highly regarded as fighters. They were sent to the region to provide defense and protection to area settlers and travelers from raiding Apaches, Comanches, and outlaws.

One of the areas regularly patrolled by Companies B and K of the Tenth Cavalry was Indian Hot Springs. The site was a well-known crossing from the United States into Mexico and back for Indians as well as cattle and horse rustlers. Nearby, a crude redoubt had been constructed to house the soldiers patrolling the region.

During the night of October 27, the seventeen Apaches who fled the Tres Castillos massacre crossed the Rio Grande and spotted the encampment of the cavalrymen. A few minutes past dawn the next morning, a contingent of soldiers was riding across a nearby ridge overlooking the hot springs and adjacent valley when the Apaches, who were waiting in ambush, attacked. During the fight, five cavalrymen were killed—William Backus, Carter Burns, Jeremiah Griffin, George Mills, and James Stanley. Two troopers were reported missing—Scott Graves and Thomas Rach. Their bodies were found several weeks later. The number of casualties suffered by the Apaches, if any, remains unknown. In any case, not a single body was found. Indians were known to remove their dead from a battle site whenever possible and provide a secret burial for them. The bodies of the cavalrymen were interred where they fell, then moved to the current cemetery during the 1960s.

Between 1925 and 1929, the hot springs, backed by a Chicago enterprise, were opened for commercial use, advertised as being helpful in curing a number of ailments including arthritis, infertility, syphilis, migraines, and tuberculosis. Rock and petrified wood found nearby were used to construct bathhouses and residences. The remoteness of the area, the rugged environment, and the poor roads, often washed out, led to the demise of the business.

During the 1950s, 1960s, and 1970s, cattle rustling in this part of Texas was still a common occurrence. Most of the stolen cattle were herded toward Indian Hot Springs where they were crossed over into Mexico, herded a hundred miles or more to the south, and sold. Three brothers who operated a nearby ranch were charged and found guilty of much of the rustling. Two of them spent time in prison and eventually were released. Since then, with the assistance of increased surveillance of the area by the US Border Patrol, rustling has all but disappeared.

Today, Indian Hot Springs is privately owned. The structures have been rebuilt and remodeled and serve as guesthouses for those who wish to experience the calming waters of the hot springs. Aside from the modest cemetery, there is little evidence to indicate the violence that took place here.

Chapter Four

The John Flynt Gang

There exists a forbidding location along a West Texas length of the Rio Grande in eastern Brewster County known as *Las Vegas de los Ladrones* (The Meadows of the Bandits). This narrow, irregular series of discontinuous *vegas* begins at a point where Maravillas Creek joins the Rio Grande and extends downstream for approximately twelve miles as the river winds its way northeastward. A companion series of vegas can be found directly across the river in the Mexican state of Coahuila.

These vegas are embraced by high limestone cliffs, occupy a valley two miles wide, and are characterized by dense thickets of *carrizo*, a tall, cane-like grass that can grow eight to ten feet tall. In addition, one finds typical Chihuahuan Desert vegetation including creosote, *lechuguilla*, yucca, sotol, mesquite, and a wide variety of cacti.

Because of the relative remoteness, aridity, and rough topography found here, these vegas have never served as a site for continuous human habitation. Today, occasional rafters, canoeists, and kayakers pass through the valley but rarely stop. The region is sometimes visited by sportsmen during hunting season.

One of these vegas is known as Flynt Vega, named for John M. Flynt, who arrived in the region during the 1880s. Flynt stocked the vega with stolen cattle, and it also served as a temporary hideout for him and his gang, a point from which they would launch their cattle rustling enterprise and conduct raids.

As the westbound passenger train No. 20 of the Galveston, Harrisburg, and San Antonio Railroad was approaching Samuels Siding in western Val Verde County on September 2, 1891, it was stopped one mile from its destination in a cut at the west end of what is known locally as Horseshoe Curve. Upon the tracks was placed a large rock that was struck by the engine. Startled, the engineer looked out of the cab and spotted another rock a short distance ahead and applied the air brakes.

As the train slowed to a stop, the engineer was surprised and shocked to see five men approach the cab, rifles in hand and pointing at him. Several shots were fired above the train. The newcomers told the engineer that they had no intention of harming him if he cooperated. If he resisted, they explained, they would kill him and the entire crew. They also explained that they were not interested in robbing the passengers, that they only wanted the shipment of Wells Fargo and Company money.

The engineer and fireman were escorted to a point fifty yards south of the train and told to raise their hands. The leader of the bandits instructed his gang members to keep the rest of the crew in the coaches, and if any attempted to leave they were to be shot down on the spot. The fireman was then ordered to accompany the leader to the messenger car where the Wells Fargo shipment was located. The fireman was told to break the windows in the side door, reach in, and unlatch it. The fireman was unable to accomplish this. Frustrated, he called to the messenger, J. Ernest Smith, inside the car and ordered him to relinquish his keys so that he, the fireman, would not be killed.

The messenger did not respond. Nor did he react to the firing of several rounds from the rifles of the bandits. Finally, a charge of dynamite was set off beneath the messenger car, but had minimal effect. When the leader announced that he had a "whole jackass load of dynamite" which he would use to blow up the car, the messenger agreed to surrender and open the door. At gunpoint, the messenger opened the safe and the bandits helped themselves to the contents, including all of the registered mail. After filling some empty mail sacks with the money and other items, they robbed the messenger and mail clerk. A moment later, the leader returned the money to the two men, stating that he was not interested in "taking a working man's money." After leaving the train, the bandits mounted up and rode south. On returning to San Antonio days later, Messenger Smith resigned from his job.

The bandits responsible for the robbery were identified as John "Three Fingers Jack" Wellington, James Lansford, Tom Fields, an unknown participant, and their leader, John M. Flynt.

A reporter for the *San Angelo Standard* (October 31, 1891) described the outlaws. Wellington was around thirty-five years of age, handsome, fair skin, blue eyes, and a "heavy, drooping mustache." The November 6, 1891, issue of the *Beeville Bee* carried an article that stated Wellington "has the instincts of a gentleman throughout. He is well posted, being conversant with Byron, Shakespeare, Longfellow, Tennyson, and other poets." Wellington's right hand had only three fingers, the rest being lost in "blasting rocks," thus the nickname. Wellington was well known to many, was rather popular, and numerous citizens expressed surprise that he was involved in the holdup. At the time of the robbery, Wellington was raising horses on a plot of land in Brewster County along the Rio Grande.

James Lansford was tall and gaunt—six-feet-two-inches and weighing only 150 pounds. He was twenty-two years of age, with a smooth face, and a "harmless, insipid appearance." Lansford was considered so docile and meek.

Tom Fields, who used the aliases Rhodes and Strode on occasion, "looks every inch the border scout." He was six feet tall, two hundred pounds, and broad of shoulder and deep of chest. He had long black hair and a heavy black mustache. He was described as a man "desperate enough for any undertaking." Fields was thirty-nine years old at the time of the robbery. Subsequent court documents suggested he was illiterate.

John Flynt was born in Gonzalez County, Texas in 1860. His father died four years later in the service of the Confederacy and his mother passed away one year after that. Flynt and an older brother were raised by an uncle who saw to their education and well-being. Flynt arrived in Brewster County no later than July 1887. That was the year in which his brand—JMF—was recorded.

Flynt was described by Texas writer Hallie Stillwell as "a handsome, well-mannered likeable young cowboy . . . a ladies man." He was six feet tall with dark eyes and a high forehead. He became engaged to Ada Fuller and the two were to be married when Flynt had accumulated enough money to support a wife and home. Men who professed to be friends of Flynt insisted that he only went along with the train robbery scheme that had been the idea of other men. Most, however, regarded Flynt as the brains behind the robbery. Texas Ranger captain Frank Jones wrote that "gambling and drinking ruined [John Flynt]."

Flynt was also known to rustle cattle. Captain Jones reported that he found stolen cattle at Flynt's camp on the Rio Grande along with several letters that proved he was "regularly in the business."

The fifth member of the gang who escaped was never identified and his fate remained unknown.

While only five men were involved in the train robbery, some area newspapers reported six, while another claimed the deed was perpetrated by "a regular army of men." The amount of money taken from the safe was reported by some as less than fifteen hundred dollars and others as fifteen thousand dollars and more.

The robbers were described as "polite, courteous, and jolly." When one of them was asked why he was compelled to rob a train, he replied that his "cattle were so poor and grass so bad that the animals were not worth skinning."

When news of the train robbery was broadcast throughout the area, Val Verde County sheriff August Kieffer formed a posse, loaded horses into a special train in Del Rio, and headed for the scene of the crime. About the same time, Judge Roy Bean in Langtry was alerted. He responded by organizing a second posse and sent them out in pursuit of the bandits. As it turned out, the trail of the robbers was not difficult to follow; it was littered with cigar butts and orange peels all the way to the Rio Grande where they crossed into Mexico.

The Bean posse, along with the Kieffer posse, stopped at the border, unsure of what to do. Instead of pursuing the bandits, they decided to await the arrival of a Texas Ranger battalion, Company D, led by Cap-

Frank Jones, Texas Ranger

tain Frank Jones. The Rangers had departed Camp Hogg near Alpine, arrived at Samuels Siding, and followed the outlaws' trail to the Rio Grande.

While the Rangers and the local posses were on the trail of the bandits, agents of Wells Fargo, along with private detectives from the Morris Detective Agency of Houston, in the company of railroad officials, arrived at Langtry. All were intent on investigating the robbery. Confusion reigned. Finally, H. H. Innes, the superintendent of the San Antonio Division of the Southern Pacific Railroad, met with a newspaper reporter and stated nothing definite was known, that rumors and "cock and bull stories" were coming in. He then said that what was known for certain was that five men robbed the train. He stated that Texas Rangers, along with some posse members, crossed into Mexico in pursuit. At some point, the robbers crossed back into Texas and re-crossed into Mexico.

The pursuit of the bandits continued for a month. As time passed, the identities of the robbers became known. A detachment of Texas Rangers under the command of Sergeant Bass Outlaw was encamped at Little Wood Hollow just outside of Marathon. From this base the Rangers scouted out into the countryside for some sign of the outlaws but with no success. As the investigation continued, it was discovered that a robbery attempt was made on a passenger train near Tesnus, a station in Brewster County, and was likely made by the Flynt Gang but aborted before anything happened.

According to author Franklin W. Daugherty, the train robbers were ultimately captured because of the discovery of a letter that had been left in one of the outlaws' camps. The letter was written to Jack Wellington by a girlfriend who lived in Val Verde County.

During the first week of October, Sheriff Keiffer received word that several suspicious characters had arrived at a store in Juno in northern Val Verde County and purchased supplies. Keiffer was convinced that the men were related to the train robbery, but he was unable to leave the county seat of Del Rio because he was required to be in court.

Instead, Val Verde County deputy sheriff Joe Sitter, along with a man named Frank Bendele, traveled from Del Rio to Juno. (Originally, the deputy sheriff's name was Sitters, but he dropped the final "s.") Their intention was to watch the house of Wellington's girlfriend in hope of apprehending him. On October 8, four men rode up to the house. While three of them waited some distance away, Wellington entered via the front door. Following a short visit, he left the house, rejoined his companions, and the four men rode away.

Sitter notified Sheriff Kieffer in Del Rio and Ranger Captain Jones at Alpine. Kieffer was tied up with court business and Jones was enroute from Alpine to El Paso by train. Sitter decided to follow the gang. He left Bendele behind to await the arrival of Jones and Kieffer. On arriving in El Paso, Ranger Jones, responding to the messages, made arrangements to transport men and horses by rail from Alpine to Comstock, all arriving by noon the following day. From here, the Rangers rode to Camp Hudson on the Devils River between Comstock and Juno. The next day, October 11, they were joined by Sitter, Bendele, and one other man. Near Beaver Lake they encountered the three-day-old trail of the bandits and found a camp where the outlaws had slaughtered a calf for food.

They followed the trail for forty miles. It wound in a northwesterly direction between the Devils River and the Pecos River. On October 13, the trackers arrived at a ranch in Crockett County known as Howard's Well. Here they discovered the bandits had passed through three days earlier. Doggedly, they continued to follow the trail through the rough country. On October 16, they came to a house on Live Oak Creek near the town of Iraan in northeastern Crockett County. Believing the bandits to be within, they surrounded the house only to find it occupied by a lone woman, She told the posse that the men they were after had departed about four hours earlier after watering their horses. They left with a man who intended to sell them some fresh mounts.

Captain Jones led the contingent northward, and three hours later they encountered the man who sold the horses to the outlaws. He told them the men they were looking for had stopped to prepare a meal just a mile up the road. Jones led his men back onto the trail and within minutes spotted the bandits. Once they were three hundred yards from their quarry, Jones ordered his men to draw their weapons and prepare to charge the camp. The bandits, unprepared, were taken by surprise.

Flynt and Wellington leaped onto their horses and fled. Fields fled on foot but was overtaken in seconds. Facing several mounted men with revolvers pointing at him, he surrendered. Lansford never made an attempt to escape.

A number of men went in pursuit of Flynt and Wellington, both parties firing weapons at one another. Wellington's horse was shot and stopped running. The outlaw jumped off and ran for cover toward a nearby hillside but was overtaken and arrested.

Joe Sitter and two other posse members pursued Flynt for another five miles when the outlaw jumped off of his horse, ran into a ravine, and attempted to hide behind a clump of brush. Sitter spotted him, and within seconds he and his fellow posse men surrounded the thicket. Sitter decided to await the arrival of Captain Jones and his Rangers before attempting to arrest Flynt.

A few minutes later, the lawmen heard a shot and ducked behind their available cover. More time passed with no more shooting, so they decided to approach the thicket. They found Flynt lying on the ground, dead. He had killed himself, they claimed, by a self-inflicted shot through his head. Lying next to the body was a hastily scribbled note requesting that all of his possessions be given to his brother, Joe. After examining the body, the lawmen found another bullet wound, one that must have been incurred during the pursuit. The bullet had entered under the right shoulder blade and went completely through Flynt's torso.

The body of John Flynt was transported back to the ranch house they had visited earlier. The next morning, Captain Jones paid the woman who lived there for a few pieces of lumber, which was used to construct a coffin. Flynt was buried not far from the house and the lawmen returned to Comstock.

On arriving in Comstock, Jones was approached by Sheriff Kieffer, who demanded that Wellington, Fields, and Lansford be turned over to him immediately. Jones refused, explaining that robbing the US Mail was a federal crime that took precedence over Kieffer's jurisdiction.

On October 23, the three prisoners arrived in El Paso by train and were placed in the El Paso County Jail. Wellington and Fields were charged with robbing the US Mail. Lansford, who agreed to serve as a prosecution witness against Wellington and Fields, was not charged, but was confined to the jail for fear that he might try to flee the country.

Wellington and Fields were scheduled to appear in federal court in April 1892. Because El Paso County Jail officials had difficulty keeping their prisoners from escaping, the two men were transferred to more secure confinement in San Antonio.

The trial commenced on April 20, 1892. Though the evidence against the two prisoners was abundant and compelling, Wellington claimed he had never before met Flynt and Lansford until several days following the train robbery. He claimed he was searching for lost cattle when he encountered them. When reminded that he was found in possession of a pistol that was taken from the express messenger, Wellington claimed Flynt gave it to him. Fields likewise testified that he met Flynt and Lansford at some point well after the robbery.

The case went to the jury on April 25. The next day, word spread that the jury was deadlocked: Ten jurors argued for conviction and two for acquittal. According to author Franklin W. Daugherty, "it was evident that a compromise had been reached." Wellington and Fields were found guilty of "robbery of the Postal Clerk W. J. Lytle of the Mails." On April 27, Wellington and Fields were sentenced to ten years of hard labor at the House of Corrections in Michigan, a federal prison. They were admitted on August 30. On November 11, 1899, they were released on "good behavior."

Some controversy about John Flynt still lingers today. Some who knew Flynt were convinced there was no way he would have taken his own life. They contended he was murdered in cold blood by the lawmen. It has been theorized that Flynt was killed just after being forced to divulge the location where the train robbery loot was hidden. The notion has also been advanced that he was killed "to protect the identity of someone who was involved in his crimes," according to author Daugherty.

Even Ranger Captain Jones was puzzled by Flynt's presumed suicide. The November 6, 1891, *Beeville Bee* quoted him as saying that Flynt "had many warm friends . . ." and that he was "young, brave, and handsome, and far away I know there was one whose heart will still be sad and lonely when she hears of his tragic end . . . ."

Some believe the fact that Flynt scribbled out a note regarding the disposition of all of his possessions is evidence enough that he killed himself. Not necessarily—Flynt could have done so thinking he might soon die at the hands of the lawmen.

To further confuse this issue, Ranger Captain Jones, in a report to the adjutant general, stated "struck trail of train robbers 75 miles north of Del Rio and overtook them 50 miles north of Howards Well and killed John Flynt and captured Wellington, Lansford, and Fields." Thus, Jones contradicts himself. In a subsequent letter to General Mabry, Jones wrote that Flynt "ran about eight miles, and after being wounded, blew his brains out."

The obvious question is: Of Jones's three communications, which, if any, is the truth?

Further controversy exists about the identity of the fifth participant in the holdup. It was clear from eyewitness testimony that five men were involved, but only four accounted for. The fifth man, according to Captain Jones, "took to the hills on foot." His identity was never revealed by the three prisoners and remains a mystery to this day. It has been suggested that the authorities knew who the fifth man was but, according to Daugherty, "chose not to reveal his participation."

Controversy piles up. It was never determined exactly how much money was taken from the Wells Fargo express messenger. Early estimates advanced the figure of fifteen thousand dollars. By the time the dust had settled, most agreed that it was thirty-six hundred dollars, though rumors of fifty thousand dollars circulated widely. The amount of money found on Flynt and the prisoners totaled $1,198. It is unknown how much of that may have been Wells Fargo money and how much were their personal funds. Following the sentencing of Wellington and Fields, $1,274.24 was returned to Wells Fargo. Fred Dodge, the Wells Fargo agent, stated that fourteen hundred dollars was returned to the company, leaving twenty-two hundred unaccounted for.

In a statement to Dodge, Lansford said the robbers were sitting around a campfire dividing the money when they spotted the Texas Rangers in the distance. During the ensuing scramble to get away, they hid most of the money. Lacking time to even dowse their fire, they fled to a nearby hill and sheltered themselves among the rocks. From their hiding place two hundred yards away, they watched as the Rangers arrived at their campsite, investigated, and then rode away.

When they were certain the Rangers were gone, they rode back to the campsite. In a curious statement, Lansford said they "found that the currency had all burned and the silver was discolored." Lansford further stated that one thousand dollars in silver had been taken during the robbery "and most of that was in their possession when they were captured."

It strains logic to make sense of Lansford's reference to the notion "that the currency had all burned." If they hid the money, as he previously stated, then how did it get burned? Surely they didn't hide currency in the campfire. And most certainly, the Rangers, assuming they had found any of the currency at all, would not have tossed it into the fire. Lansford's comments do little more than add another layer of mystery to what happened to the bulk of the robbery take.

Going on the assumption that the robbers hid or buried the currency and silver during their flight, many have searched for it. One of the searchers was Bass Outlaw, a Texas Ranger who rode with a posse pursuing the bandits. During the time he served, as well as after he was dismissed for drinking and gambling while on duty, Outlaw retraced the pursuit route and dug holes all along the way hoping to recover the loot. His labors proved fruitless, and many are convinced that the money remains cached somewhere along the trail followed by the train robbers.

Conversely, there are those who believe some or all of the buried treasure has been recovered. A Brewster County rancher named Travis Roberts told author Daugherty that, "some of the money was recovered by a man named Hammond." Hammond, whoever he was, was known to be a dogged searcher for the buried loot, and his brother-in-law was convinced that he found some of it.

Texas ranch woman and author Hallie Stillwell also told Daugherty she had been informed that one of the bandits, either Wellington or Fields, returned to Marathon following his release from prison, borrowed a horse from the Gage ranch, and rode out to some point along the escape path followed by the bandits and recovered "his share of the loot."

Banditry was not unknown in the Texas-Mexico border area during these times, but it remained low key and confined to specific areas. The dramatic train robbery by the Flynt Gang, along with the prolonged pursuit involving a variety of law enforcement agencies, propelled the boundary-related lawlessness into the public eye as a result of newspaper coverage. Unfortunately for those living along the Rio Grande, both on the Texas and Mexico sides, things were about to get worse.

CHAPTER FIVE

Shootout at Pirate Island

DURING THE MID-NINETEENTH CENTURY, RESIDENTS OF THE WEST Texas borderlands had much to be concerned about. Hostile Indians still roamed the area and conducted raids on outlying ranches. Attacks near the outskirts of town limits were not uncommon. Mexican bandits crossed the Rio Grande and preyed on travelers and settlers with impunity. Rattlesnakes, as well as poison-rich scorpions, spiders, and centipedes, were a constant threat. As if that were not enough to be concerned with, the weather often lurked as a potential threat.

The arid trans-Pecos region of Texas served up malevolent weather on occasion. Daytime temperatures of 115 degrees Fahrenheit during the summer were not uncommon. Springtime winds tore across the desert at speeds of up to seventy miles per hour and more, carrying loads of sand and dust and driving residents indoors for days at a time. Winters could be unbearably cold, and dry frigid winds from the north cut through garments and chilled to the bone. The sparse rainfall in far West Texas—six inches per year or less—made agriculture difficult before the onset of irrigation, and what few crops were raised were generally confined to the land adjacent to the river courses.

In spite of the aridity, there were occasions when the rain fell in great quantities in only a few hours, often causing flash floods which inundated livestock and claimed the lives of the luckless and unwary who happened to be caught in arroyos and canyons. The environment, along with the weather, like Indians, bandits, rattlesnakes, and scorpions, was unpredictable, never constant, and often threatening.

During the spring of 1854, the weather grew menacing. For several days the winds blew strong, transporting tons of West Texas sand and dust. Traveling was kept to a minimum, the blowing sand stinging the eyes of man and horse alike. Visibility was sometimes reduced to twenty feet.

Following the winds of that year, an unusually high number of thunderstorms moved into the region, dropping rain with a regularity heretofore unknown to those who lived there. Residents along the Rio Grande Valley from El Paso to the tiny settlement of Indian Hot Springs one hundred miles downstream could not recall a time when it had rained so hard for so long. In the desert where the rain is considered a blessing, farmers and ranchers were growing concerned at the amount of water falling. Before long, the narrow ephemeral streams that laced the barren desert floor were swollen with runoff, overflowing and flooding surrounding areas. As excess water from the surface and tributaries rushed into the Rio Grande, the principal drainage artery for West Texas and parts of northern Mexico, the channel filled and water spilled onto the vast floodplain for miles. With the increased flow came increased velocity. Great chunks of soil were torn from the banks and carried away with the current as the river carved new meanders.

During the peak of the Rio Grande's flooding, a freak occurrence took place along a portion of the river channel southeast of San Elizario, Texas. Here, the river broke through a low bank and scoured out a new route that flowed for two miles south of the original Rio Grande. This new channel flowed for six miles before reconnecting with the original. The next day when the rains ceased and the river levels lowered, residents noted the Rio Grande had established a brand new route via the southward meander, leaving a portion of Mexico six miles long and two miles wide between the old channel and the new. Because the old channel still contained water, the isolated strip of land was for all intents and purposes an island, and was thereafter referred to as such.

This was not the first time the Rio Grande manifested the potential to form a new course. During a period that ranged from 1829 to 1831, heavy rains caused the river to overflow its banks, cutting a new channel that ran south of the floodplain on which perched the Mexican towns of Ysleta, Socorro, and San Elizario, "thus placing them on an island some twenty miles in length and two to four miles in width," according to historian W. H. Timmons. Area residents called the swath of land *La Isla*—The Island.

The Treaty of Guadalupe Hidalgo in 1848 stated that the international boundary should follow the deepest channel. As a result, American officials declared that the southern channel was the deepest and therefore was the legitimate route of the Rio Grande. Thus, Ysleta, Socorro, and San Elizario were now determined to be within the jurisdiction of the United States. Though Mexican officials lodged a number of protests, they all proved futile.

The isolation of yet another strip of land in this area as a result of the 1854 rains and subsequent flooding was soon to create additional problems. This unusual event led to a situation that frustrated law enforcement officials in both the United States and Mexico. Because this new island was still technically part of Mexico, it was therefore deemed outside the jurisdiction of the United States. Furthermore, the Mexican authorities found it inconvenient to administer the area, because the new channel of the Rio Grande separated it from the rest of the Mexican state of Chihuahua and no bridge provided ready access.

This twelve-square-mile piece of isolated land was inhabited by a family named Holguin. The acknowledged leader of the clan was Jesús María Holguin, who had been described as a ruthless killer. The Holguins had lived there for several generations and over time earned a reputation as violent criminals. They were known to have led horse-stealing forays both into Mexico and the United States, and they had long been suspected of preying on travelers making their way along the San Antonio–El Paso Road.

Now that their habitat was insulated from law enforcement on both sides of the border, the Holguins began to operate their criminal empire with more impunity and bravado than before. As a result, other locally notorious bandits and drifters were attracted to the stronghold, which eventually came to be known throughout the area as Pirate Island. Now, more than ever, the Holguin-led bandits terrorized the surrounding country on both sides of the river, stealing livestock and killing any and all that would stand in their way. During the period of three years since Pirate Island had been formed, it was estimated that the bandit population grew to nearly seventy-five.

Robbery and harassment of travelers along the San Antonio–El Paso Road by the Holguin gang increased. Livestock was not safe when the Holguins were on the move, and stolen cattle and horses were sometimes spotted on the island. Murder was common. After decades of predation and atrocities, area residents grew disgusted with the continued feeble attempts of local law enforcement authorities and appealed to the State of Texas to assign the Rangers to clean up Pirate Island. The year was 1893.

The relationship between the Texas Rangers and citizens of Mexican descent was never good. The Mexicans often charged the Rangers with wanton killing, and during raids by squads of Rangers, the innocent as well as the guilty were often randomly gunned down. Charges of ethnic discrimination flew. The events of the El Paso Salt War in 1878 did little to endear the Texas Rangers to Mexicans and Mexican Americans living along the river. During the fifteen years that had elapsed since the Salt War, tensions had abated somewhat. When the Holguins learned that a contingent of Texas Rangers was on its way to Pirate Island, however, the bitter feelings were renewed.

During the spring of 1893, Texas Ranger captain Frank Jones received orders to move into the area now called "San Elizario Island" and put a stop to the ongoing robberies and killings. As he researched the history of the region, Jones discovered that the Holguin family, as well as others residing on the island, were part of the gang that murdered three of the principals during the Salt War confrontation. He also learned they were responsible for the capture and harassment of a platoon of Texas Rangers that had been assigned to bring an end to the Salt War.

Jones, along with a contingent of five Texas Rangers, arrived at San Elizario during the middle of June 1893. Jones and his men spent several days scouting Pirate Island from the other side of the river. The ranger captain soon recognized the strategic superiority of the location. He also determined that dozens of men, presumably bandits, were living there, along with their families, in a small village that consisted of a cluster of squat adobe houses near the middle of the island.

Jones decided it was imperative to arrest Jesús María Holguin and his son, Servicio. He believed that if he removed the leader of the bandit clan, the rest would disperse. In a move that defied logic, Jones and his five Rangers, outnumbered ten to one, ignored international law, crossed the northern channel, and rode onto Pirate Island.

Within minutes, the Rangers spotted two Mexicans on horseback fifty yards away and gave chase. The Mexicans rode straight toward the village and, on arriving, yelled to the others that the *rinches* were attacking. The two dismounted and secluded themselves in one of the houses. Either unable or unwilling to invoke common sense, Captain Jones and his Rangers rode straight into the center of the village where they were immediately fired upon by gunmen shooting from the concealment of a number of houses.

Rather than turn and flee, Jones panicked and, in a bizarre decision, ordered his men to dismount and return fire. Within seconds, Jones was struck in the chest by a large caliber bullet. He died instantly.

When Jones went down, two of the Rangers regained their horses, remounted, and fled back to the border. The three remaining Rangers, their horses having bolted during the firefight, turned and followed on foot. During the retreat, the rearmost Ranger was shot in the back and killed.

The sound of the gun battle attracted more Mexicans who lived in a small settlement on the south side of the Rio Grande. Mounted and armed, they crossed the river and charged into the Pirate Island village to provide reinforcements. On determining what had taken place, they set out in pursuit of the hated Rangers, who were fleeing for their lives.

The four surviving Texas Rangers managed to cross the old channel to safety. Without stopping, they fled straight to San Elizario, a mile-and-a-half to the west. On arriving, they telegraphed El Paso for help.

Around noon of the following day, a contingent of thirty-five Texas Rangers arrived from El Paso and rode to the crossing at the old river channel. A single scout was sent ahead into the village on Pirate Island to demand the return of the bodies of Captain Jones and the second dead Ranger. By coincidence, a company of Mexican soldiers entered Pirate Island from the south. The scout and the soldiers arrived in the middle of the village at the same time.

The island residents were uncooperative. On their own, the Mexican soldiers located the body of Captain Jones, loaded it onto a spare horse, and announced they would deliver it to the waiting Rangers. What happened to the body of the second Ranger was never learned.

As the Mexican soldiers were making their way toward the Rangers, they encountered Jesús María Holguin and three members of his gang. Following a brief shootout, all four outlaws were captured alive.

After leaving the body of Captain Jones with the Rangers, the Mexican soldiers transported Holguin and his three companions to the jail at Juarez where they were placed in a cell. The four outlaws were never seen again, and no record of their fate has ever been found. With the disappearance of bandit leader Holguin, the depredations emanating from Pirate Island decreased dramatically. After the passage of a few more months, they ceased altogether.

Ranger patrols continued to frequent the border between El Paso and several miles downriver, with special attention given to Pirate Island. With the passage of more time, the area was deemed safe and the patrols ceased.

Today, Pirate Island is indicated on US government topographic maps as San Elizario Island and is located south of the small farming community of Fabens. Dozens of descendants of the Holguin family continue to live on the "island" and in San Elizario.

Chapter Six

Chico Cano, Border Bandit

It can be reasonably argued that the most well-known border bandit was a man named Chico Cano. His fame and notoriety as an outlaw was the result of the tales—some true, some not—told of him by ranchers and soldiers from the Texas side of the river, as well as by the Texas Rangers. Cano's role and reputation as a bandit arose not from any desire on his part, but from his sense of survival. Cano was born in Mexico in an environment where people were shaped, as author Elton Miles said, "by need, hunger, and mistreatment," all of which drove some of them to robbery and murder.

Miles quoted a soldier who was stationed near the border as saying, "Although I am gunning for Mexicans constantly, I feel that I too would be a bandit if I were treated as some of these people have been treated." Border rancher Evans Means once stated, "Just mean white men did more meanness than the Mexicans."

Whatever his real name was, the man who was to become one of the most famous border bandits of all time was called Chico since he was a toddler growing up in and around Pilares, Mexico, as well as its sister village, Pilares, Texas, on the north side of the river. The word *chico* can mean boy or small. The name stuck, and he was forever after known as Chico. Elton Miles advances the notion that the word *chico* means scarred. Miles relates that when Chico and another youth were roughhousing in the waters of the Rio Grande, the father of the boy was under the mistaken impression that Chico was trying to drown him. The

Chico Cano

father pulled a knife, jumped into the water, and slashed Chico's throat. The nonfatal wound left an ugly scar. While a good story, most doubt its authenticity, and outside of Miles no one has ever heard of using the term "chico" to indicate a scar.

Joyce Means, daughter of Evans, recorded much of the history of the region. She wrote that Chico Cano did not want to kill anybody, but he would fight to protect what little he owned. Cano became a legend along the border. He and his brothers—Manuel, Jose, Antonio, and Robelardo—undertook small raids across the border into Texas to steal cattle, horses, saddles, food, and clothing, all to outfit his band. Several have argued that Cano and his band were simply retrieving cattle that had originally been stolen from the Mexicans by Anglo ranchers.

Cano fought with the army of Venustiano Carranza as well as Pancho Villa. As a soldier, he crossed the Rio Grande at will; he fought with Carranza's army as well as Villa's and held rank in both. Having gained a reputation as a feared border bandit, he was wanted on both sides of the Rio Grande. Cano was intelligent and always seemed able to outsmart his enemies, and both Texas and US authorities blamed him for nearly every act of violence in the Big Bend region of Texas during the first two decades of the twentieth century.

Cano was born in 1884. He was described as tall, big chested, and always wore a gun on his hip. Unlike most Mexicans, he had a ruddy complexion and was said to look like an Irishman. He was an excellent shot with rifle and revolver and a capable and dependable cowhand. As a youth, he took a job on a ranch near the Pecos River in Texas where he broke and trained horses. Cano was the only Mexican on the crew and received insults and abuse from the Anglo cowboys. He often got into fights, and he always won. Tired of such things, he moved to Pilares, Mexico, and established a small ranch at San Antonio del Bravo across the river from Candelaria, Texas. Here, Cano captured and broke wild horses, raised and sold cattle, and made ropes and saddlebags from the fibers of the ubiquitous lechuguilla that grew in the area. It was often said but never proven that the horses and cattle he acquired were stolen from ranchers on the Texas side of the river. It soon got to the point

Venustiano Carranza

where whenever livestock was reported missing, Chico Cano and his brothers were invariably named as suspects even though they may not have been within fifty miles of the theft.

Following the onset of the Mexican Revolution in 1910, Texas residents near the border grew concerned, even paranoid, about the potential for violence to spill over, about banditry and possible raids on their homes and livestock. Mexicans living near the Rio Grande were no strangers to hard times, but the Revolution created even greater hardships. They were often reduced to eating cottonseed and the pads of prickly pear cactus. To provide meat for their families, some wandered north of the river and stole cattle. Furthermore, followers of Villa and Carranza were known to conduct raids into the United States to procure horses for their military and cattle for food. Also targeted were trading posts and ranch houses where there was a possibility of acquiring firearms and ammunition.

As the number of livestock thefts increased on the US side, more often the finger was pointed at Cano. That Cano and his band stole cattle and horses is undisputable. What is also indisputable is that in many cases he was stealing cattle back from Texas ranchers who had earlier rustled the cattle from ranches in Mexico.

In at least one case, Cano was assisted by a Texas rancher who ultimately double-crossed him. A Sierra Vieja rancher, whose name is disputed, assisted Cano in smuggling horses out of Mexico and hiding them in a canyon near Van Horn, Texas. When it appeared that the rancher was determined to be a person of interest in a number of smuggling schemes, he decided to portray himself as a good citizen and reported Cano to lawmen in Valentine, Texas. Overhearing this report, another rancher, one sympathetic to Cano, sent word to the bandit what had transpired, providing him sufficient time to flee back to Mexico. By the time a squad of Texas Rangers arrived at the canyon, Cano was long gone.

Joe Sitter was a former deputy sheriff and Texas Ranger working as a US Customs inspector. Sitter despised Cano and devoted his life to capturing or killing him. When two of Sitter's neighbors reported the loss of thirteen horses taken by four Mexicans, he immediately blamed Cano and set out to find him at his home in Pilares, Texas, where he was living at the time.

Sitter arrived in Pilares, Texas, on January 23, 1913, during a wake for a child who had died. He was accompanied by two men—Jack Howard, a US Customs inspector, and J. A. Harvis, an inspector for the Texas Cattle Raisers Association. Cano was attending the wake and playing accordion in the home of Nicomedes Martinez where the body was laid

Joseph Sitter

out and several mourners were conversing. Most of those in attendance were Cano's brothers. Sitter pounded on the door. Grabbing his rifle, Cano slid under the table upon which the body of the child was laid out. When Martinez opened the door, Sitter demanded that Cano be sent out. If not, he said he would set the house on fire. Martinez requested a minute to deliver the message and closed the door. Cano's brother, Robelardo, disguised himself by dressing in women's clothes. When Martinez reopened the door, he asked that the woman be allowed to leave the house. Sitter agreed, and the brother scurried out and hastened toward the river. After crossing into Pilares, Mexico, he searched for and summoned the other brothers and made plans to rescue Chico.

In the meantime, Chico, not wishing to be responsible for the destruction of a neighbor's house, surrendered to Sitter. He was handcuffed, placed on a mule, his feet tied together under the animal's belly, and led away. No one believed for one moment that Cano would be allowed to live. The Texas Rangers were widely known for killing their prisoners outright and offering the explanation that they were forced to shoot the captives as they were attempting to escape.

In the meantime, in Mexico Robelardo found Manuel. The two quickly assembled a small band consisting of Lino Baeza, Jose Jimenez, Juan Sauceda, Francisco Zapata, Roman Robeledo, Entimio Zalgado, and Chico Jimenez. The gang hastened back across the border into Texas and headed for Pilares Pass to intercept Sitter and rescue Chico.

On arriving at the Pass, Sitter, his two companions, and Chico Cano were spotted by the Mexicans who waited in hiding. As the riders rounded a bend in the trail, the rescuers opened fire. Their main target was Sitter. They knew well that he would kill Chico at the first opportunity in the event of a rescue attempt. Sitter was knocked from his saddle, a bullet wound to the head. Harvis was struck in the leg, and Howard was shot through the stomach. Howard's wound was mortal, but he would live for several more hours.

At the first volley of gunfire from the Mexicans, the mule upon which Chico was tied bolted toward a dense cluster of mesquite trees. Initially this had the potential for a dangerous, if not deadly, predicament. If the hobbled Cano slid sideways off the mule, he would have been kicked to death by the hooves. If he managed to stay aboard the mule, he might have been cut to pieces by the sharp, long thorns of the mesquites. As luck would have it, Jose Jimenez, who leaped upon his mount after the initial barrage of gunfire, raced toward Chico and caught up with him only a few yards from the mesquite trees and managed to turn the mule.

With Chico, the Mexicans raced back across the Rio Grande. With some difficulty, they managed to remove the handcuffs. This done, Chico swatted the mule on the rump, sending it back across the border. He told his companions he did not want to be accused of yet another theft.

Having heard the sound of gunfire coming from Pilares Pass, residents from the Texas Pilares went to see what had transpired. Finding the three wounded men, they brought a wagon, loaded them into it, and carried them to the little store in town. Howard was in extreme pain, spitting up blood, and it was clear he would not survive. He died at 7:00 p.m. the following day. Sitter and Harvis were transported to Hotel Dieu hospital in El Paso where they were treated and held for thirty days. The entire time Joe Sitter lay in the hospital bed, he thought of nothing but seeking revenge against Chico Cano.

Jim Howard, brother of the slain man, somehow learned that Manuel Cano had pulled the trigger on the weapon that killed him and swore to get even. Jim Kilpatrick Jr., brother-in-law to Howard, also vowed vengeance. Across the border in Mexico, Chico Cano likewise swore an oath to seek retribution against Joe Sitter.

Two weeks later another raid took place, this one at the Lee Hancock Ranch fourteen miles northeast of Alpine, Texas. This was followed by another raid on the Lawrence Haley Ranch. During both raids, horses, saddles, weapons, ammunition, food, and clothing were taken. Following the raids, the bandits fled south into Mexico. Though he was never spotted, everyone throughout the area was convinced the leader of the raiders was Chico Cano.

On February 23, 1913, Mexican president Francisco Madero, along with the vice president José María Pino Suarez, were killed in a coup d'état led by General Victoriano Huerta, who immediately seized the office of the presidency. Huerta had enemies among the country's military generals, three of whom began organizing revolts in an attempt to overthrow him.

General Pancho Villa

The generals were Pancho Villa, Venustiano Carranza, and Emiliano Zapata. Fighting raged throughout the Mexican countryside.

On December 10, 1913, Villa attacked the Mexican town of Oji-naga sixty-five miles downstream from Pilares. Learning of the activities in Ojinaga and the subsequent flight of many of that city's residents, who were forced to abandon their homes and property and most of their belongings, Chico Cano grew concerned. Following the month-long battle in and around Ojinaga, Villa crossed the border and was seen in El Paso, Valentine, Marfa, Shafter, and Presidio. Villa's increasing movements near Cano's homeland began to trouble him. He was concerned that a future attack on towns such as the Mexico Pilares would likewise cause the residents to lose their homes and property. Chico felt a responsibility and determined that he must become involved in what he had long sought to avoid.

On August 15, 1914, Carranza's forces marched into Mexico City and occupied it, forcing President Huerta to flee the country. A short time later Carranza was installed as president of Mexico. Carranza proved inept at running the country and further generated the ire of Villa. Carranza suspected Villa of coveting the presidency and attempted to minimize his influence. He refused to acknowledge Villa's contribution to the causes of the Revolution and withheld his appointment to a senior position in the government.

On September 23, 1914, Villa publicly denounced Carranza and vowed to move against him. In November, Villa formed an alliance with Emiliano Zapata and increased his activities devoted to overthrowing the new government. Battles and skirmishes escalated and moved closer to Chico Cano's territory of Pilares, Mexico. The now famous border bandit decided it was time for him to make a stand against threats to his community, to his people. His attention was now focused on the happenings in northern Chihuahua and his presence in Texas diminished to almost nothing. For a time, Texas residents relaxed, hoping the raiding days of Chico Cano were over. They weren't. Chico Cano would ride again when the time was right.

On May 13, 1915, a Villista camp near Pilares, Mexico, was raided by twenty-five men under the leadership of Chico Cano. One of Villa's captains, accompanied by seven enlisted men, had entered Pilares and confiscated a number of horses belonging to the citizens. A short time later, Cano was located and informed of the act. Cano, intending to recover and return the horses, lost no time in gathering his men and racing to the camp. On arriving, the raiders opened fire on the surprised soldiers who responded in kind. Shooting between the two factions continued for twenty-four hours before Cano decided it was time to depart. When he and his men rode away, they left two soldiers and one mule dead. They also took forty of the horses in possession of the army, almost all of which they had at the time.

Within a few days, Captain Howard R. Hickok, commander of Troop B, Fifteenth Cavalry, was ordered to coordinate with Mexican *federales* to jointly patrol the area along the Rio Grande in hopes of locating Cano and placing him under arrest. As it turned out, they had no success. It was clear to Hickok that the Mexican army was not interested in encountering Cano.

On May 21, Cano's old nemesis Joe Sitter, in the company of five other men, departed Valentine, Texas, for Pilares, Mexico, to investigate a report of stolen horses. Sitter eagerly looked forward to the assignment, for he longed to return to the border and have another attempt at trying to kill Chico Cano. He saw this assignment as his opportunity.

On May 22, Sitter and company were camped near a spring seven miles from Pilares. In a brief conversation with some of Villa's soldiers, Sitter learned Cano and several other bandits were hiding in these same mountains on the Texas side of the border and that they held a large herd of smuggled horses and mules.

On the morning of May 23, Sitter and his companions came across the tracks of the bandits and the horse herd not far from their campsite. A short time later they spotted several of the horses in question in the foothills of the mountain range. The animals were guarded by three of Cano's men. The Americans engaged the rustlers but lost them in the winding canyons of the range.

That night as Sitter and his companions lay in their bedrolls, they became aware of a herd of horses passing close by and Mexican herders speaking in loud voices, apparently unaware of the Americans. Sitter claimed one of the voices belonged to Chico Cano. When dawn broke, Sitter and his men saddled their horses and followed the trail of the bandits, which led into a deep canyon.

One of Sitter's fellow riders, J. E. Vaughan, expressed the opinion that it was too risky to venture into the canyon. He implied that Sitter was on a mission to kill Cano and would jeopardize the lives of his fellow riders for the opportunity to do so. Sitter told Vaughan to go on home if he wanted to, so he left.

On the morning of May 24, Sitter and his remaining four companions rode into the mountains southeast of Porvenir to a spring near a location called the Coal Mine Ranch. Convinced that Cano and his band were a short distance ahead, Sitter divided up his party. Three of the men rode into the canyon to make an attempt at seizing the horses. Sitter and Texas Ranger Eugene Hulen climbed a nearby hill to observe.

Unknown to Sitter and his party, Cano had set a trap. He left the horses where they could be seen to entice Sitter and his bunch to approach while Cano and his men lay in ambush. The three riders were fired upon but not hit, and they sought shelter immediately. Lying in hiding and under fire for four hours, the three men finally broke away and fled to the location where they had last seen Sitter and Hulen. Not finding them there, they continued their flight on foot, dodging the bullets of the bandits all the way.

The three fleeing men, all suffering from thirst as a result of having no water, finally arrived at a water hole where they encountered their pack animals. They rode them to the McGee Ranch five miles away. From there they sent a message to the John Poole ranch another six miles further requesting help. When the message arrived, John Poole, who had a telephone, called authorities. Before long, eleven men arrived at the Poole Ranch by automobile. They carried their saddles and using borrowed stock mounted up and went in search of Sitter and Hulen.

They arrived at the entrance to the canyon where the horses had been kept, and there they found the bodies of Sitter and Hulen. From the evidence nearby, it was apparent that the two men held off the Mexicans in a firefight for some time before succumbing. Sitter was found lying in a fetal position with his hands covering his face. His head had been caved in by a large rock and his fingers had been broken, apparently while he was trying to protect himself. He had eleven bullet holes in his body. It was clear Sitter had died a painful death. Even Sitter's horses had been shot to death. Clothes, boots, watches, money, and weapons all belonging to Sitter and Hulen had been taken by the bandits. According to the reports that were filed, Chico Cano was blamed for the murders.

Within a few days, Texas's Governor Ferguson demanded to know how one bandit could cause so much turmoil and show up his Texas Rangers the way he did. Ferguson authorized a ten-thousand-dollar reward for Cano, dead or alive, and demanded immediate action. Ferguson dispatched Texas Ranger captain Monroe Fox to Marfa to assemble and lead fifty Rangers to the Rio Grande. US Army Troops A, B, C, and D of the Thirteenth Cavalry were also sent from Fort Bliss to a variety of locations near the border.

On June 18, a meeting was held in Fabens, Texas, and was attended by members of the Thirteenth Cavalry, Texas Rangers, a number of county sheriffs, and even a member of General Villa's Secret Service. The objective was to run down and eliminate Chico Cano and his band of outlaws, now estimated to number in excess of one hundred men. Cano was placed on a wanted list released by the Department of Justice.

Several days later, Revolutionary general Pancho Villa sent a colonel to meet with Cano and his men at Pilares. Villa considered this location important to his efforts and authorized his representative to enlist Cano and his men into the army, by force if necessary. If they refused, stated the colonel, Villa would attack and destroy not only Pilares but several neighboring communities as well. Cano refused, telling the colonel to go to hell.

A short time later, a representative of Carranza's army met with Cano with similar demands and threats. Cano's response was the same as the one he presented to Villa's emissary. Now, to protect his people from possible depredations by the various armies, he led the entire population of Pilares and surrounding areas to a location 160 miles upriver to a location known as Bosque Bonito. Cano decided to align himself with another Mexican general, Pascual Orozco, whose army opposed both those of Villa and Carranza.

Carranzistas attacked Bosque Bonito with the intention of seizing it, but Cano's men defeated them easily. Cano was awarded the rank of

BORDER BANDITS, BORDER RAIDS

colonel in Orozco's army. In late August or early September, Orozco, along with five of his men, was shot to death by a sheriff's posse. With Orozco, his army, and his finances now out of the picture, Cano decided it was best for his people to abandon Bosque Bonito.

During the last week of November 1915, Fort Bliss lieutenant George S. Patton received a telegram from General Pershing purporting that Chico Cano and a band of two hundred armed and mounted riders were approaching Sierra Blanca, Texas, for the purpose of raiding the town. Patton placed troops stationed at the town on alert. He issued orders that the bandits were to be intercepted and either captured or chased back south into Mexico. As it developed, Cano never attacked the town and the soldiers never saw a single bandit.

A US military report dated December 4, 1915, stated that Cano had joined Carranza's army and was given command of fifty men stationed at the Mexican town of San Antonio del Bravo, just across the river from Candelaria. Cano was given the rank of captain.

The months and years rolled along. Cano remained active rustling cattle and horses on both sides of the border, always managing to stay just out of reach and out of sight of the US Army and the Texas Rangers. Cano was growing older, and growing weary of the confrontations with those who would try to end his rustling and banditry ways. He was slowing down and longed for a more peaceful life. He and his wife were raising children, and he wanted them as far from the fray as he could manage.

By 1937, Chico Cano was fifty years old and living on his ranch in the mountains in Mexico not far from the border. His banditry days were mostly over, the members of his gang either dead or dispersed. He had been idle for so long that it appeared he was no longer wanted or hunted. That was fine with him, for he enjoyed the relatively quiet life on his ranch near Cedillos, Mexico.

During the spring of 1941, Cano was out on his ranch herding some cattle to a pen where they were to be branded. Instead of the normal mule he rode for such chores, he selected a freshly broke young horse, one that was somewhat skittish and nervous. Cano felt the horse needed the work and the experience. As he was herding the cattle toward the pen, a heifer broke loose from the herd and headed in another direction. Shaking out a loop from his rope, Cano pursued the animal and tossed the loop. As he did so, the heifer turned and ran back to the herd. At the same time, the young horse somehow got its legs tangled up in the rope, causing it to panic. It bucked wildly and threw Cano onto the ground where his head struck a rock. He was knocked unconscious.

Minutes later, the spooked horse rode past the house where it was spotted by Cano's wife, Teresa. She summoned son Chico Jr. and the two hitched up a wagon and drove it back along the tracks made by the horse until they found Cano. Still unconscious, he was loaded into the wagon and carried to the tiny village of Guadalupe where he was delivered to a Dr. Castañeda. The physician treated Cano and suggested he be moved to a hospital in Juarez. Cano resisted, but his wife and sons insisted. He was taken to the Clinica Belén in Juarez where he remained for twenty-eight days.

It was rumored that during the time Cano was under the care of Dr. Castañeda, a group of Americans offered the doctor a significant amount of money if he would poison the famous bandit. It was also rumored that while he was at the clinic in Juarez that at least one attempt was made on his life. Either because of the assassination plot or the drudgery of lying in a hospital bed for days on end, Cano demanded to be released and taken back to Guadalupe. There, he would remain with an old friend Ramon Jimenez and be near the company of several of his trusted gunmen. Cano was warned before he left the clinic that he might not live long without the proper treatment. After a few days at the clinic, he returned to Cedillos.

During the following days, it was becoming clear that Cano was having trouble remembering people and places and that his health was failing. He died on August 28, 1943. He was fifty-six years old. As it turned out, it was not the head injury that caused his passing. Cano was suffering from stomach cancer that, in turn, led to cardiac arrest. He was buried in a small cemetery in a remote, rugged area at the end of a rocky path and not far from the Rio Grande.

To the Texas ranchers, Texas Rangers, the US Army, and other law enforcement agencies, formal and otherwise, Chico Cano was a bandit, an enemy. To the people of Mexico, however, he was seen as a friend, a defender, a savior, and today in the somewhat restricted geographic area along several miles of the Rio Grande along the Texas-Mexico border, he is regarded as a folk hero.

Chapter Seven

Brownsville Train Robbery

After fording the Rio Grande from Mexico on October 18, 1915, a party of some fifty raiders (estimates range as high as one hundred), some on horseback and some on foot, traveled to a point known as Tandy's Crossing near a trestle bridge three miles north of Olmito Crossing. Some claim that the Mexican raiders were joined by a number of Mexican citizens living on the Texas side of the border.

Olmito was six-and-one-half miles north of Brownsville, Texas. Here, the raiders busied themselves with preparations to derail a St. Louis, Brownsville, and Mexico Railway train. The bandits were led by a man named Aniceto Pizano, according to some researchers. Pizano was a rancher in Cameron County, Texas.

Area resident J. L. Allahands said the raiders removed the spikes and angle bars from a rail on the west side of the tracks. A stout wire was fastened to the rail, the wire then stretched a short distance away and tied around a shovel handle. There, the raiders hid in ambush. A short time later the train was spotted coming down the track at thirty-five miles per hour. Just before it arrived at the point where the rail had been tampered with, three of the raiders, pulling on the shovel, jerked the rail aside, causing the engine to jump the track and hit the ties whereupon "it was ditched and thrown at right angles to the main line." When the engine tipped over, the engineer was killed and the fireman injured. Behind the engine, the baggage car and mail car toppled over on their sides.

When the train finally stopped, the raiders fired their weapons from hiding, and then advanced upon the two passenger cars that were carrying several soldiers along with Anglo, Mexican, and black passengers. Within moments, four raiders, carrying rifles and revolvers, entered the first of the passenger cars, yelling and screaming curses as they shot at passengers who were trying to find shelter between the seats.

Dr. Edgar S. McCain (sometimes reported as Dr. Eugene Shannon McCain) and a former Texas Ranger named H. J. Wallace ran for what they presumed was the safety of the bathroom at the end of the passenger car. They were followed by a teenage Mexican who was also a passenger. The raiders hammered on the door of the latrine with the butts of their weapons and ordered the passengers out. When the door opened, one of the raiders grabbed the Mexican boy and pulled him out. Firing into the latrine, one of the bullets struck Wallace in the shoulder. McCain suffered a mortal wound when he was shot in the abdomen.

The bandits ran through the cars yelling, *"Matan los soldados y Americanos cabrones!"* Kill the soldiers and the American bastards! Three American soldiers were killed and five more wounded. The Anglos and blacks were robbed of cash, jewelry, and whatever they carried in their suitcases, but the Mexicans were spared. Following the robbery, the bandits returned to the brush and made their getaway. During their flight toward the south, they burned the trestle bridge.

The robbery was effectively and efficiently carried out and not a single bandit was killed or injured.

At the time, what has been called the Brownsville Train Robbery was described as "the boldest raid yet by Mexicans into United States territory." To this date, no one knows precisely who the bandits were or if they claimed some affiliation, military or otherwise, although US Army general Frederick Funston insisted Emiliano P. Navarette, the mayor of Matamoros, was the instigator and that the bandits were shouting, *"Viva Carranza!"* The extent of the Carranza army's involvement in the raid, as well as other border difficulties in this region for which he was blamed, if true, have never been ascertained, and Funston's observations have never been verified.

Texans wanted retribution for the raid and demanded immediate reaction. State newspapers were filled with demands relative to eradicating the "mangy wolves," the "lice in the thickets," and the "hounds of perdition," all references to the Mexican-American residents of the South Texas region. The festering racism rampant in this region exploded with a fury and many a frustration was taken out on innocent Mexicans, some with disastrous results.

A deputy sheriff led a posse of armed men into a field where some laborers were harvesting a crop and shot eleven of them down for no reason other than that they were Mexican. It was later determined they had no connection to the train robbery whatsoever. Six additional Mexicans "suspected" as being involved with the robbery were pursued and shot down. A band of Texas Rangers encountered four Mexicans on a road they traveled and hung them from a nearby tree "as exemplary punishment." Some Mexicans encountered in the area during the time period immediately following the robbery were arrested and held for trial. Relationships between the Mexican and Anglo denizens of the lower Rio Grande Valley deteriorated rapidly and remained hostile for years.

A number of explanations were advanced to explain the reasons for the train robbery. Dr. Rodolfo Rocha, a history professor at the University of Texas—Edinburg, and an authority on the Rio Grande Valley goings-on during the early 1900s, says the banditry associated with the train robbery, as well as other outlawry in South Texas during this time, was a form of social protest against injustices committed against working class Mexican Americans. Others suggest that the motivation for the robbery, as well as for some of the other criminal activities, was simply banditry turned loose. Still others insist the bandits were Carranzistas who were accumulating money with which to purchase arms and ammunition for the ongoing Mexican Revolution. The truth is, historians, professional and amateur, cannot agree on the reasons for the train robbery.

Rocha refers to the train robbers as "social bandits," and that the robbery was a "spillover from the Mexican Revolution," that the raiders were "expressing frustrations with the social conditions" in the Rio Grande

Valley and were "influenced by the ideology of the . . . Revolution, which was the movement of landless [peasants]." Rocha points out that many of the Mexican-American citizens living in the Rio Grande Valley were subjected to intense abuse by Anglos.

In the end, none of the actual bandits involved in the robbery were ever apprehended, nor were any motives or affiliations made clear. Tensions ran high along the border for years, and fear of another raid pervaded the Anglo communities. It was a long time before things settled down, but not much time passed before other cross-border raids were undertaken.

CHAPTER EIGHT

The Columbus Raid

ONE OF THE FEW INCURSIONS INTO THE UNITED STATES FROM MEXICO that did not involve Texas took place on March 9, 1916, when a band of Villista troops raided Columbus, New Mexico. Columbus was, and still is, a small town on the border sixty miles west of El Paso, Texas. The population in 1916 hovered around three hundred men, women, and children and in the town could be found two hotels, a post office, a bank, and several stores. The town did not have electricity; most of the lighting was supplied by kerosene lanterns. The streets were unpaved, and when the spring winds blew dust and sand filled the air. Immediately south of the town ran the east-west route of the El Paso and Southwestern Railroad. Columbus served as a watering stop for the railroad.

A number of sources describe the attack on Columbus. They vary in length, quality, and content, and many are contradictory. Thorough and intense examination of the available materials yields the following account.

To this day, a number of mysteries surround this raid. There is no consensus on the total number of Mexican soldiers who participated in the attack though most researchers placed it at slightly less than five hundred. While it was clearly Villa's forces that attacked the small town, a handful of writers have insisted that Villa himself was not present. Debate continues to swirl as to the motives for the raid.

By 1916, Pancho Villa was regarded as a fugitive from the regime of Mexican president Venustiano Carranza. Following two encounters with

Carranza's army in Celaya and Agua Prieta, Villa was soundly defeated. The general retreated into the interior of the Mexican state of Chihuahua where he disbanded his demoralized army, keeping only five hundred of his most loyal and devoted followers.

Without governmental support, Villa's once powerful force was reduced to raiding and looting to procure food, arms, ammunition, and supplies. They became little more than a guerrilla force of bandidos. Along the US–Mexico border, almost every raid was attributed to Villistas, whether they were present or not.

Villa was born Doroteo Arango in 1878 in the Mexican state of Durango. Fleeing from the servitude imposed on his family by a wealthy *hacendado*, the young Arango took to the nearby Sierra Madres getting by any way he could. This sometimes included banditry. In time, he took the name Pancho Villa, a once notorious outlaw who roamed this same area.

When the idealist Francisco Madero proposed a revolution to liberate the *peones* from the tyrannical reign of Mexican president Profirio Diaz, Villa volunteered to assist, bringing his band of some fifty hardened riders to the effort. For years, Villa terrorized Diazistas, in particular Don Luis Terrazas, whose large cattle ranches and estates covered most of the Mexican state of Chihuahua.

During the late winter of 1916, Villa and his forces were desperate for provisions and were running low on ammunition. Already in northern Chihuahua near the US border, Villa decided to attack Columbus, New Mexico.

In the middle of the village of Columbus was a store owned by two brothers, Sam and Louis Ravel. Over time, Villa had done business with the Ravels, purchasing guns and ammunition. Some researchers suggest that Villa paid the Ravel brothers a considerable amount of money for a shipment of guns and ammunition that he never received. Sam Ravel refused to sell Villa the guns, but also refused to return the money. The raid, therefore, may have been motivated by revenge as well as acquiring more loot and supplies, according to researchers.

Still others insist that it was necessary for Villa to keep his slowly disintegrating army active to keep it together. Already, some of his soldiers had defected to Carranza's army, and many simply deserted, preferring a return to their labor in the fields to the tedium of riding and marching endless days with little action.

Others believe Villa wanted to send a message to the hated Americans because of their support for President Carranza, and for providing Carranza arms and ammunition that were used to defeat Villa and his troops in previous battles. Heading this rationale was the notion that one of Villa's intentions was to stop the train that ran from El Paso, Texas, to Douglas, Arizona, for the presumed reason that among the passengers on that train were the lawyers Luis Cabrera and Roberto Pesqueira, who had provided assistance to his enemy, Alvaro Obregon. The train was never molested. Attached to this was the additional theory that, because the United States recognized and supported Carranza, Villa wished to make a point that he still held power and was a force to be reckoned with.

Yet another reason for the raid was proposed. Immediately south of Columbus across the railroad tracks was Camp Furlong, an encampment housing the Thirteenth Cavalry. Here could be found a supply of weapons, including machine guns, which Villa desperately needed.

Throughout the years, a few have interpreted the Columbus raid as being inspired by the German government to distract Americans and hopefully prevent them from joining the Allied powers in World War I. While German influence in Mexico, and in particular with Villa, was significant, there exists little evidence to support the notion that they assisted in choreographing the raid.

Another theory held by only a few was that the US government was behind the raid as an attempt to generate war sentiment and occupy Mexico for tactical maneuvers. Like the previous theory, this one carries little credence.

Author Manuel A. Machado Jr. has offered the opinion that Villa's vanity led to the raid on Columbus. Machado argued that "the idea of oblivion did not appeal to the man who had dominated the Mexican scene for so long," and that Villa wanted his presumed power and leadership to be noticed, particularly by the United States.

Any of the above reasons for attacking Columbus were plausible, and over the years each was invoked to one degree or another. In the end, however, most agree that the raid planned by Villa was primarily designed to acquire loot, arms and ammunition, and much needed supplies and provisions as well as fresh mounts.

On the other hand, Mexican historian Roberto Blanco Moheno wrote that Villa's raid on Columbus was his "most stupid, irresponsible action." Moheno regarded Villa as a madman who suffered from epilepsy who committed the "act of a jackass."

As Villa and his force moved across northern Chihuahua, on March 7 they encountered seventeen cowhands working on a ranch near Rancho Boca Grande, thirty miles across the border and southwest of Columbus. The American foreman, Arthur Kennedy, was killed along with the cook. The rest of the cowhands, all Mexicans, were made prisoners. In response, the captives agreed to join up with Villa, who returned their arms and made them part of his army.

In the meantime, US Army general John J. Pershing received intelligence that Villa and an army of some fifteen hundred men were moving across northern Chihuahua with the intention of attacking Juarez across the Rio Grande from El Paso. Scouts for the Thirteenth Cavalry spotted Villa and his army fifteen miles west of Palomas, a Mexican village directly across the border from Columbus. (The town on the border was and is called Palomas. Another village, named Las Palomas, is eight miles south of the border.) The scouts estimated Villa had between three hundred and four hundred men with him. (Records show that Villa's army consisted of 485 men.) Colonel Herbert J. Slocum, the commanding officer at the army camp, was so convinced that Villa and his men would continue on toward Juarez that he left the camp for Deming, New Mexico, thirty-two miles to the north.

Some information received by the military indicated that Villa might try to cross the border and surrender to the Americans. Other

General John J. "Black Jack" Pershing

sources suggested Villa's intent was to cross the border and raid small American towns.

On the morning of March 8, Juan Favela, the foreman for the Palomas Land and Cattle Company, rode to Camp Furlong to alert Colonel Slocum that he had spotted Villa's army fifteen miles south of the border

Col. Herbert J. Slocum

below Palomas. Villa was using this location as a staging area for his men. Slocum, who had by then returned from Deming, was unconcerned.

During this time, Villa's army controlled the border area west of Juarez, and he felt he was in total control. Villa' movements were not furtive; Villa, convinced that the forces of his enemy Carranza were too diminished to pose any kind of threat, brazenly led his troops throughout the area for all to witness. Villa was correct.

On March 8, Villa sent two of his officers to scout Camp Furlong and Columbus. While he was awaiting word from his scouts, Villa discussed with his other officers the possibility of attacking Columbus and the military camp. Later that day, the scouts returned and reported that only thirty soldiers were at the fort and that they, the scouts, were not even challenged when they rode through. At 4:00 p.m., Villa's Colonel Candelario Cervantes led an advance guard of eighty troops out of the camp toward Columbus. The rest of the army followed behind.

Columbus, New Mexico, consisted of a cluster of adobe houses, a few wood frame buildings, two hotels, several business establishments, and a railroad station. Camp Furlong was south of the east-west running railroad tracks.

At 1:00 a.m. on the morning of March 9, Villa's army reached a large arroyo where they halted for a time. A short time later, they reached the border at a point two-and-a-half miles west of the official crossing at Palomas where sixty-five troopers and two officers were stationed. Here, they cut the wire fence, passed through the gap, and rode slowly, deliberately, and as quietly as possible until arriving at a point some five hundred yards south of the railroad tracks. Here, Villa outlined to his officers the plan for the attack.

Colonel Candelario Cervantes was to proceed with a detachment of eighty men in a line as skirmishers. They were to travel just to the west of Coot's Hill and occupy the knoll. General Pablo Lopez was to lead one hundred men and form a skirmish line to the left of Cervantes, then follow the railroad track into town. Colonel Nicolás Fernandez was to lead a line of sixty skirmishers to the left of Lopez and attack the Americans from the north. General Francisco Beltran was to lead his contingent of

125 men to form up to the left of Fernandez and also attack from the north to envelop the Americans. General Juan Pedrosa and his forty men in reserve, along with Villa, would remain with the horses.

It has long been debated whether or not General Villa was actually in the area of the Columbus raid, some reports stating that he was as far away as Ciudad Chihuahua. The battle plan described above, reproduced in the official papers of General John J. Pershing, should settle the controversy once and for all. It is also important to note that a number of people were witnesses to Villa's presence, including Mrs. Maude Hawk Wright, who had been Villa's prisoner for ten days prior to the attack.

According to research conducted by Villa scholar Dr. Haldeen Braddy, at the estimated time of 4:15 a.m., Villa's army formed a line of skirmishers facing east. Villa is reported to have yelled, "*Váyanse adelante, muchachos!*" Go forward, or attack.

The sound of gunfire erupted, shattering the silence of the desert night. Private Fred Griffith (also recorded as Griffin) was standing guard near regimental headquarters when he spotted several Mexican horsemen. Griffith ordered them to halt, and they responded with a fusillade of rifle fire. Griffith was mortally wounded, but managed to kill three of the raiders. The Villistas surged forth into the military camp and then into the town, shouting "*Viva Mexico!*" "*Viva Villa!*" and "*Muertan los gringos!*" while shooting at doors and windows.

All of the officers of the Thirteenth Regiments were off the post save for Lieutenant James P. Castleman, the officer of the day. As per regulations, they had all of the arms and ammunition locked inside the guardhouse. The surprised enlisted men were forced to break the locks to secure the weapons. Once they were armed, the soldiers had difficulty identifying the enemy in the dark. Further, the Benét-Merciér machine guns they had been provided proved complicated and difficult to operate, jamming repeatedly. The lightweight weapons had a heavy recoil, causing consistent accurate aiming to be a problem.

The medical corpsmen locked themselves in the camp hospital, refusing to take part in the fight raging without. When soldiers with the machine guns attempted to enter the hospital to repair a broken machine gun, the medics refused to open the door. Meanwhile, another contingent of raiders stormed into Columbus, entering it from several different directions. The town was ill prepared to defend itself against the Villa army and was taken completely by surprise.

By the time the raid began, a handful of cooks had already arrived at the mess shack and were busy with preparations for breakfast. Brewing atop the wood-fueled stove were several large pots of steaming black coffee. As the fighting grew outside, a number of raiders attempted to seek cover inside the cook shack. After breaking down the door and charging inside, one of the cooks tossed a large cauldron of scalding coffee onto the invaders, and another cook waded into the group of Mexicans swinging an axe used to chop firewood. Several of the attackers were killed. They were later identified as Yaqui Indians. Yaquis made up a significant portion of Villa's soldiers.

The contingent of Villistas that skirted the military camp and rode into town penetrated as far as the Commercial Hotel halfway up Main Street. In downtown Columbus, the screams of women and children could be heard above the sound of gunfire. Milton James was helping his pregnant wife to what he perceived to be the safety of the Hoover Hotel when he was struck down by a bullet, mortally wounded.

Lieutenant Castleman, barefoot, ran out of the Officer of the Day quarters and right into a Mexican raider. The raider fired his rifle at the officer and missed from only three feet away, burning Castleman's face from the blast. Castleman shot and killed the Villista soldier.

As the US soldiers became fully aware of the raid, their training kicked in and together they laid down a withering fire of shooting, advancing on the raiders as they did so. The Mexicans were startled by the sudden and effective resistance of the soldiers, whom they figured to surprise and overcome with little to no difficulty. Castleman's riflemen gradually battled their way through the camp and into the town, killing several Mexicans in the process.

According to reports of eyewitnesses, commanding officer Colonel Slocum never became involved in the defense of Columbus or Camp Furlong. According to resident Jack Thomas, the colonel hid in a barn owned by a Mr. White. The colonel later received a severe reprimand for his lack of preparation and involvement. Though Slocum was later exonerated by an Army Board of Investigation, he was never promoted to a higher rank.

The raiders appeared intent on locating the Ravel brothers. On arriving at the Ravels' store, they broke down the door and found fourteen-year-old Arthur Ravel and his brother Louis sleeping in a back room. The invaders demanded Arthur open the safe, but the lad told them he did not know the combination. They dragged Arthur out of the building and over to the Commercial Hotel where they thought they might find Sam Ravel, the owner. Ravel, however, was in El Paso.

Following a few moments of milling around on Main Street on their horses, a number of Villistas dismounted and ran into the Commercial Hotel and raced up to the second floor where the guests were sleeping. Longtime hotel resident Steven Birchfield opened his door and, in precise Spanish, told the raiders that they could have all of his money. He withdrew a number of bills and coins from his pocket and tossed them onto the floor. As the bandits fought over the money, Birchfield crawled out a window, down a fire exit, and to safety.

Another guest at the hotel, Walton R. Walker, married for less than two months, was torn away from the embrace of his wife and shot to death on the stairs. The raiders looted his pockets, decapitated him, and then set his body on fire.

Two other residents—Dr. H. M. Hart and Charles DeWitt Miller—were escorted out into the street and shot to death.

William T. Ritchie was the owner of the Commercial Hotel, and he and his wife and three daughters lived on the second floor. Several raiders burst into the Ritchie quarters and ordered the man into the street. His wife pleaded for him not to leave them alone, but he followed the orders. When he reached the lobby the raiders demanded his money. He gave them all he had on his person—fifty dollars—and was immediately shot and killed. Other bandits ransacked the Ritchie room and even pulled rings off of the fingers of the females.

Across the street from the Commercial Hotel was the Lemmon and Romney grocery store. Several raiders emptied cans of kerosene across the wooden building and set it afire. James Dean, a grocery merchant, attempted to run across the street and was shot down, his body riddled with bullets.

Other raiders entered the Commercial Hotel and dragged out three men and a woman. They shot the three men and were about to kill the woman when she shouted *"Viva Villa!"* They let her go, but decided to set fire to the building. Two of the raiders decided to take Arthur back to the store, but on the way, they were shot dead. By this time, the Commercial Hotel was roaring with flames. The light from the fire illuminated many of the raiders. The Villistas shot volleys into any home or building that showed a light, in the process killing a number of citizens.

Columbus citizen A. B. Frost placed his wife and three-month-old baby in their automobile and backed it out of the garage in preparation to flee from the developing gun battle. Just as he accelerated, he was struck by a bullet. Badly wounded, he steered the car onto the road toward Deming when he was shot again. Unable to continue driving, he was moved into the backseat by his wife, who took control of the vehicle and continued on to Deming.

Having repaired and mastered the operations of the machine guns, Lieutenant John Lucas led several troops into Columbus, catching the raiders in a crossfire. At 5:30 a.m., Colonel Slocum arrived. He directed Castleman to hold the town on the east. By this time, dawn was breaking over the horizon and the Mexicans, not expecting such heavy resistance, began to disperse and the attack disintegrated. On the outskirts of town a few minor skirmishes took place, but the Villa forces were largely in retreat, driving horses taken from Camp Furlong's stable ahead of them. From a hill southeast of town, Villa and his reserve force covered the retreat. On their way out of town, the raiders stopped at the camp and took a quantity of food and supplies as well as eighty cavalry horses, thirty mules, and three hundred rifles.

By the time the Columbus raid was over, a total of eighteen Americans had been killed—ten civilians and eight soldiers. Six soldiers and two civilians were wounded. The bodies of ninety Mexicans were found. One report states that twenty-three were wounded, but how this number was arrived at is unknown. According to Castleman's report, five were taken prisoner. Forty cavalry horses were killed during the raid as well as a number of the animals ridden by the Mexicans. The dead Villistas were piled up in a vacant lot, their bodies set afire.

Major Frank Tompkins assembled a contingent of troopers and set off in pursuit of the fleeing Villistas. He was soon joined by Captain Smyser with his Troop H. The force crossed the border and had proceeded about three hundred yards into Mexico when they were fired upon by a platoon of Villa's troops from a low hill. Tompkins and his force charged the hill, forcing the Mexicans to retreat. Once he had taken the hill, Tompkins sent a courier back to Columbus to obtain permission for the US Army to continue pursuit. A short time later he received a message from Colonel Slocum to use his own judgment. Tompkins pushed on.

An hour later, Tompkins and his troops overtook the main body of raiders. Smyser's forces, joined by Lieutenant Castleman's, overtook the main body of raiders. But the Americans were subjected to heavy rifle fire, with Tompkins receiving a wound in one knee. Making a stand, the US Army poured heavy fire into the ranks of the Mexicans, forcing them to flee deeper into the country. Tompkins again resumed the chase and caught up with the raiders once again. This time, however, the Mexicans assembled at a prime vantage point from which they launched a counterattack. Greatly outnumbered, Tompkins withdrew and made preparations for another attack. Eventually deciding that he was at a distinct disadvantage—low on ammunition and without food and water—the major finally called for a retreat and led the force back across the border.

Some historians maintain that the army was lucky to have fought off the Villista raiders as effectively as they did. Writer I. J. Bush referred to the army's defense as a "fiasco" and cited a report that commanding officer Slocum, having attended a party in Deming, was drunk and "incapacitated." Major Frank Tompkins was identified as a coward by Mexican historian Alberto Salinas Carranza. It was recorded, however, that Tompkins participated in the rout of the attackers and was a member of the party that pursued them into Mexico.

The Villista attack on Columbus provoked the US government to the degree that they now opposed Villa's position in Mexico. Once regarded by the US press as a heroic revolutionary, he was now treated as little more than a madman and a bandit.

CHAPTER NINE

The Glenn Spring Raid

GLENN SPRING IS JUST EAST OF THE CHISOS MOUNTAIN RANGE IN BIG Bend National Park and in the shadow of Chilicotal Mountain, elevation 4,108 feet. Glenn Spring feeds water into a draw that has its origins in the Chisos and cuts across the desert, incising its way through the multi-colored clays and other sedimentary rock. During the 1870s, the spring was enclosed by a low rock wall and was an important source of water for cattlemen who lived in the area. Today, as a result of long abandonment and the dense growth of cattails and cane, it is difficult to find.

The flow of water from the spring trickles down Glenn Draw for a mile before sinking into the soft bottom of the channel. The place is quiet, peaceful, the only sound often being the hum of insects and rustling of brush and grasses by the wind. Paleo-Indians lived here as evidenced by the prehistoric artifacts and rock art found nearby. It is difficult to believe that on May 5, 1916, this pleasant section of the desert-mountain area was the home of nearly eighty residents, a factory, and a cavalry camp, as well as the setting for a bandit raid that left near total destruction and four dead.

Glenn Spring is located along one branch of the old Comanche Trail, a route taken by these plains Indians on their way into Mexico to conduct raids for horses, women, and slaves. The first Anglo to establish residence in the area was H. E. Glenn, who grazed horses here during the 1870s. Glenn cleaned out the spring and constructed the rock wall that remains today. Not long after settling nearby, Glenn was killed by Indians.

Throughout this part of the Chihuahuan Desert grows a plant called candelilla, or wax plant. Candelilla (*Euphorbia antisyphilitica*) is a low-growing perennial that sports hundreds of pencil-thin gray-green stems that grow vertically from the base. The highly prized wax from this plant, which coats the stem and protects the plant from drought, was used for shoe polishes, car waxes, chewing gum, phonograph records, candles, adhesives, lubricants, anti-corrosives, and for waterproofing canvas tents, a vitally important product during World War I.

In 1914, C. D. Wood and W. K. Ellis perceived the vital need for wax and connected it to the abundance of candelilla plants in the Big Bend region. At Glenn Spring, they constructed a factory to separate the wax from the plant and prepare it for shipping. The stems were boiled in large vats of water. Sulphuric acid was added to facilitate the separation of the wax from the stems. When the wax floated to the surface, workers skimmed it off and subjected it to a second boiling to remove any impurities. Following a cooling period, the wax was cut or broken into blocks and packaged for shipping. Workers were paid one dollar per day.

The Glenn Spring wax plant employed between forty and sixty workers at various times, and hired C. G. Compton to operate the general store and post office that had been established in the makeshift town that people referred to as Glenn Spring. The store stocked food and items necessary for the Mexican population that arrived in the area to work. At the end of the day, the Mexican workers returned to their *jacales* on the opposite side of Glenn Draw.

On May 4, Wood, along with his wife, Julia, and their small son departed for Alpine in response to rumors of an impending raid. Cavalry captain Caspar W. Cole of Troop A had passed along information that a band of "Villa bandits" had massed near Ojinaga for the purpose of conducting raids into the Big Bend country.

At 11:00 p.m. on the night of May 5, 1916, C. G. Compton responded to a knock at his door to find a Mexican he did not know on the doorstep. The man asked how many soldiers were at the tent encampment located a few hundred yards to the southeast. Compton informed the nocturnal visitor there were nine, a sergeant and eight privates. A short time later, a number of riders arrived at the edge of town. (Reports differ with estimates ranging from sixty-five to four hundred, with most researchers in agreement that the force consisted of from sixty-five to seventy-five men.) They dismounted, readied revolvers and rifles, and then advanced on the general store from three sides, firing their weapons. From information obtained by the military, the raiders intended to "kill the soldiers, burn the candelilla works, steal all the horses they could find, and plunder the store and houses."

According to Captain Cole, the gang of bandits was made up of both Villistas and Carranzistas as well as some of the Mexicans who lived on the Texas side of the border. Allegedly, as the bandits attacked some of them yelled *"Viva Villa!"* while others cried *"Viva Carranza!"* It is questionable whether these bandits were loyal to either Mexican general, and a number of researchers have concluded that the raid was solely for the purpose of robbery. While it has never been verified, many believe Chico Cano was one of the leaders of the raiders.

When the shooting started, Compton fired back from the windows of his house. His nine-year-old daughter was screaming in fright and proved to be a distraction. Compton's two sons somehow remained asleep. The daughter begged Compton to take her to the home of one of his employees, a woman who did their wash. After calming the little girl down, he put her on his back and raced the one hundred yards to the woman's shack where he deposited her. Compton then headed back to the house to rescue his sons.

Before he could return to the structure, however, Compton was pinned down by gunfire between the boiler room and the blacksmith shop. He was unable to advance, and from his position, he watched the drama unfold between the attackers and the cavalrymen.

At the first volley of shots, C. K. Ellis and his wife fled to a nearby canyon, and then walked twelve miles to the ranch of John Rice. The trek must have been difficult, for Ellis had a wooden leg.

Seven of the cavalrymen were sound asleep when the attack came. One man, in uniform, was posted as a sentry. In Captain Cole's report, he claimed that the sentry spotted the arrival of the bandits and fired several shots from his revolver to awaken and alert his fellow soldiers. Following the sentry's volley, says Cole, the bandits started their attack and began shooting.

As the bullets started flying, the sentry took refuge in the cook shack and another soldier hid in the tent where forage for the horses was stacked. After grabbing their weapons, three cavalrymen ran from the sleeping tent and joined their comrade in the cook shack while the rest ran for the forage tent. The gun battle raged for another three hours.

Around 3:00 a.m. the raiders noted that the roof of the cook shack was dry-thatched with boiled-out candelilla stems. They tossed kerosene-soaked rags onto the roof, setting it afire. The dry thatch burned quickly and hot. Inside the shack there was no water with which to fight the fire, and before long the burning embers were falling on the heads and shoulders of the soldiers within. When they could stand it no longer, the troopers broke from the building. Private William Cohen, who was climbing out of one of the windows, had the entire top of his head blown away by a shotgun blast. Private Stephen Coloe dashed out the front door, his clothes on fire. Bullets struck him in the head, chest, and shoulder. Private Hudson Rogers ran out the front door and managed to flee from the building. As he raced across the desert, his burning clothes provided a target for the raiders. Rogers was gunned down one hundred yards away, a bullet through the head. Private Roscoe Tyree was trapped inside the house, remaining there until the raiders departed hours later. The burned men who survived sported large blisters on their bodies. In the end, three soldiers were killed and most of the rest wounded.

Sergeant Smythe was the last to leave the burning building. He was unhit as he fled for cover in the nearby hills. The soldiers in the forage tent also managed to make it to the sanctuary of the hill, from which they fired upon the bandits.

Compton was able to leave his hiding place near the boiler room but only made it to a position behind a large rock. From this position, he watched as the store was looted. The store appeared to be the primary objective of the raiders. They took everything except for the sauerkraut, which they thought was spoiled food, and large bags of flour and corn-meal, which were difficult to transport and would have slowed down their escape.

From his home two miles away, Wood could hear the sound of the battle. At first, he thought it was nothing more than the celebration of the Mexican holiday, *Cinco de Mayo*. On spotting the glow of burning buildings, however, Wood and a neighbor, Oscar de Montel, grabbed their rifles and set out in the dark toward the commotion to determine what was going on. Wood was no stranger to armed combat. He was a retired Army infantry officer who had fought in both Cuba and the Philippines during the Spanish-American War. The two men arrived at the tail end of the gun battle and estimated around sixty raiders were involved. They were immediately fired upon and took shelter behind some rocks and waited for daybreak.

While the store was being looted, the post office was robbed of money. Following this, a number of the raiders, carrying the stolen goods, departed. The rest, however, went about the task of rounding up the cavalry horses, as well as the mounts belonging to Compton and Ellis. While Compton was hiding behind the rock, raiders entered his home and looted it. Before entering the house, a bandit called out. When there was no answer, he fired a shot through the front door. The bullet ricocheted and struck Compton's five-year-old son, Tommy, in the heart. (At least one account lists the boy's age as seven.) The other son, a deaf-mute, was unharmed.

Around 7:00 a.m., according to Compton, the last of the raiders departed, heading south toward the Rio Grande. They left behind one of their dead. Compton found several pools of blood, and estimated that a number of the raiders had been badly wounded.

As Compton and Ellis stood on a rise above the tiny village of Glenn Spring and looked down upon the destruction, they wondered if peace would ever return to this once quiet and serene location.

Around mid-morning on Saturday, the regularly scheduled replacement cavalrymen arrived from Marfa and took in the scene. The troopers loaded the bodies of the dead soldiers, along with the wounded, into a wagon. Though injured, Sergeant Smythe refused to go. Ellis and Compton, along with Compton's surviving son, joined the returning soldiers, arriving at Marathon where the wounded were treated.

At dawn Sunday morning, Captain Cole received telegraph orders from military headquarters in El Paso to assemble his troops and meet up with Brewster County sheriff Allen Walton's automobile posse of twenty men including civilians, Texas Rangers, river guards, ranchers, and cowhands at Marathon. From there, the caravan traveled the one hundred miles of extremely rough and rocky roads to Glenn Spring, arriving eleven hours later at 5:30 p.m. They were about to embark on a pursuit and rescue mission that would take them into Mexico in violation of international treaty.

The village of Glenn Spring suffered heavy losses: four dead, four wounded, the store and post office looted, buildings burned, and most of the wax plant destroyed. With the plant able to operate only on a limited basis, most of the Mexican workers and their families moved away.

At the end of World War I, the demand for, as well as the price of, candelilla wax dropped dramatically. In 1919, both Ellis and Wood sold their properties to a rancher named Burcham. After Ellis and Wood departed, so did the rest of the Mexicans.

Little remains at the site of Glenn Spring to suggest there was once a thriving village and an important industry here. A few of the original building foundations can be seen, along with remains of corrals constructed by a succession of ranchers. The spring, one of the reasons people came to this area to begin with, still flows, still providing a modicum of water to this section of the desert.

Chapter Ten

The Boquillas Raid

On the night of May 5, 1916, eighty men bent on robbery and murder arrived at the south bank of the Rio Grande near San Vicente, a tiny Mexican village ten miles southeast of Glenn Spring. Seventy-five of the riders under the leadership of Rodriguez Ramirez, a colonel in the Villista army, proceeded northwestward toward Glenn Spring. The remaining riders, led by Lieutenant-Colonel Natividad Alvarez, also a Villista, turned toward the northeast and followed the river along the Mexican side toward the settlement of Boquillas. Across the river from the Mexican Boquillas was a small village on the Texas side, also called Boquillas.

As Alvarez led his followers along the selected route in the moments just before dawn, he spotted a man walking among a herd of thirty cattle. The raiders drew their revolvers, then rode up and surrounded him.

The man was Monroe Payne, a tall, ruggedly built black man who had crossed the river earlier to check on a herd of cattle he grazed on the Treviño Ranch near San Vicente. The bandits robbed Payne of what little money he had, beat him, and then took him prisoner, forcing him to accompany them.

Payne was a Seminole-Negro, the son of a Seminole scout for the US Cavalry, and raised in a Seminole settlement near Musquiz, Coahuila. During the Indian Removal policy of the 1830s, a number of eastern tribes were displaced from their lands in the Carolinas, Georgia, and elsewhere and marched west to Indian Territory (now Oklahoma), along a series of routes referred to as the Trail of Tears. During one of these treks, a number of Seminole-Negroes escaped and fled south, crossing into Mexico and establishing successful ranches in Coahuila. He had cowboyed on the Buttrill Ranch in the Rosillos Mountains and now worked on the Treviño Ranch.

Payne was a man of mystery, and a bit of legend surrounds him. It has been told that as a youth he entered the army of Porfirio Diaz, the president of Mexico. After the onset of the Mexican Revolution, he left and joined the forces of Venustiano Carranza where he rose to the rank of colonel. Some have claimed that Payne received a pension from the army as a result of being badly wounded. He moved to the Big Bend region and raised goats. When Payne was in need of money, it was said, he sometimes returned to Mexico where he hired out as a gunman to protect cattle herds from rustlers.

As the sun came up, the five Mexican raiders and Payne arrived at Boquillas and headed straight for the Deemer Store. Payne worked at the store on occasion for owner Jess Deemer. On arriving, the bandits found Deemer inside. On seeing the raiders' weapons and noting that Payne was a captive, Deemer realized they were bent on robbing the business, Deemer offered no resistance and stood aside as the bandits emptied the shelves and the cash register. Deemer later stated that he even helped the bandits load some of the goods into his own wagon.

Knowing that no help would arrive at the store in this somewhat isolated location, the bandits took their time packing stolen goods and loading them onto their horses. Around 10:00 a.m., they were joined by several companions who had just ridden in from the raid on Glenn Spring. Some have insisted that Chico Cano was among them, but this notion carries little to no evidence.

When they were ready to leave, the raiders took Deemer and Payne with them, along with another sometime employee named Pablo Alcala, and crossed the Rio Grande into Mexico. Deemer was forced to drive his own wagon filled with stolen goods. Monroe Payne was forced to walk behind the wagon. It has been written that some of the bandits wanted to kill Deemer, but others argued that he be spared for the numerous kindnesses he was known to have provided for Mexican families on both sides of the river.

As the raiders passed through Boquillas, Mexico, they split up. The group that included the prisoners Deemer and Payne continued on ahead. The other group rode to the headquarters of the nearby Puerto Rico Mining Company, an American-owned silver mine. Shortly after crossing the river, they had spotted a truck coming from the mine and heading toward the river. At a prescribed destination, the truck driver and another man unloaded items from the truck at which point the bandits, who had lain in hiding, approached. They forced the men to drive the truck to the mine headquarters while the bandits lay down in the back.

At the headquarters, the bandits, weapons at the ready, stormed the office and the company store, which they proceeded to loot. In the process, they discovered the mine payroll, which they took. After taking a watch from Carl Halter, the mine superintendent, they went to the several nearby houses, the homes of mine employees, and sacked them. This done, and considering the possibility of pursuit by American military, they took eight more prisoners, including Halter, and the mine physician, Dr. Homer Powers. (Some accounts claim Powers was taken captive at Deemer's store when he returned from treating a patient in Terlingua, forty miles away to the northwest.)

All of the loot taken from the mine was added to the goods stolen from Deemer's store, and loaded into the truck. After making certain the vehicle was oiled and filled with gasoline, they traveled southward. One of the prisoners was ordered to drive. Powers, Halter, and two other prisoners were instructed to ride in the truck. Alvarez told Halter that their destination was Torreon. Once there, he said, the prisoners would be released and sent back to Texas. Before leaving, Alvarez decided to send some of the raiders back to Deemer's store to procure extra supplies, mostly food.

The driver, realizing all of the Mexicans were ignorant of the capabilities of the truck, drove very slowly, allowing most of the raiders to get as far ahead as possible. When the riders ahead were out of sight, the driver purposely stalled the engine, claiming it had overheated and that it was necessary to let it rest for a while before it could be started up again. While they waited under a guard of seven men, they planned an escape.

Later while driving through a sandy area the truck got stuck. The driver explained that it would be necessary for the raiders to help them push the vehicle out of the sand trap and then for some further distance to get it started. The driver explained how this was done, and the Mexicans gathered near the rear bumper, laid their rifles on the ground, and began pushing. Three other prisoners assisted them. Unknown to the raiders, the driver depressed the clutch and slipped the transmission into reverse. When the bandits had managed to generate significant speed from pushing the vehicle, the driver released the clutch, causing an abrupt stoppage of the truck. The surprised Mexicans were knocked to the ground. As confusion reigned, the Americans jumped the raiders, seized their weapons, and killed four of them. The rest were taken captive and held at gunpoint. One of the captives was Alvarez. The Americans, along with their prisoners, marched back to Boquillas, Texas, where the raiders were turned over to the Brewster County sheriff on May 8. The bandits were later tried and sentenced to life in prison.

Captain C. W. Cole received information that the raids on Glenn Spring and Boquillas had been well planned and executed by a man named Rodriguez Ramirez, alleged to be a colonel in Pancho Villa's revolutionary force. The objective, it was stated, was to secure arms and ammunition for the army, but this remains conjecture. Ramirez's original contingent of men numbered seventeen, but was soon joined by others from both sides of the border. Ramirez had led the group of raiders that earlier attacked Glenn Spring.

On May 10, a contingent of US Cavalry arrived at Deemer's store. Their mission was to enter Mexico and rescue Jess Deemer and Monroe Payne, who were still prisoners of the raiders. In addition, they were to recover as much of the stolen goods as possible and capture the bandits responsible for the kidnappings and robberies.

The military units would travel into Mexico in pursuit of the bandits. The commanding officer, who had no experience with this part of Mexico, expected it to be an easy mission, but soon discovered that the terrain south of the river provided far more challenges than anticipated.

While the subsequently filed official report claimed the mission was a success, the expedition, described in the following chapter, was botched in a number of ways.

CHAPTER ELEVEN

US Cavalry Pursuit into Mexico

ON LEARNING THE NEWS OF THE GLENN SPRING RAID AND THE ATTACK
at the Deemer store and subsequent kidnapping, Troops A and B of the
Eighth Cavalry stationed at Fort Bliss, Texas, were ordered to the border.
In addition, Troop F and Troop H of the Fourteenth Cavalry stationed at
Fort Clark near Brackettville were mustered and told to join the A and
B troops. From Fort Sam Houston near San Antonio, the Signal Corps
was assigned to the contingent: Their job was to string a telephone line
from Marathon, Texas, to the American Boquillas.

In partial response to the raid on Columbus, New Mexico, allegedly
ordered by the revolutionary Pancho Villa two months earlier, and inas-
much as some of the Glenn Spring raiders were heard to shout "Viva
Villa" during their raid, the War Department ordered a full-scale military retaliation. According to researcher and author Arthur R. Gomez,
the army was to "track down and engage the men who committed the
'Glenn Spring outrage,'" and, if necessary, they were to follow them into
Mexico.

Colonel Frederick W. Sibley assigned Major George T. Langhorne
to command the operation. As an officer in the US Army, Langhorne
manifested a great deal more flair and style than most. He cut a dashing
figure with his stout, muscular build and carefully maintained mustache.
Langhorne has been referred to as "dapper." He would have approved
of General George Custer's flowing locks of blond hair and fringed
buckskins, and both men would have been equally at home in Buffalo

Bill's Wild West Show. Part of Langhorne's flair was associated with his Cadillac touring car, one that he drove at every opportunity with the top down and waving at people. He liked to be seen. In spite of his unusual style for a military man, he was generally well liked by his men. When he was informed of his assignment to Boquillas, Langhorne lost no time in readying his Cadillac, and his chauffeur, for the trip.

On Sunday, May 8, horses, troopers, necessary gear, and Langhorne's Cadillac were loaded into railroad cars for the 250-mile trip by rail to Marathon. They arrived at 10:00 a.m. the next day. Within an hour after the train stopped, the troopers were saddled and packed and moving in a line down the rough, winding, ninety-two-mile road to Boquillas, Langhorne in the lead. At the rear of the column came a supply truck. Several newsmen tagging along in two Ford sedans, their own automobiles, accompanied the soldiers. The trip would take two-and-a-half days. As the contingent got under way from Marathon, 110 additional cavalrymen, accompanied by a supply wagon, crossed the Rio Grande into Mexico at San Vicente. The raiders had a five-day head start on the US military. The crossing marked the first time American forces had entered Mexico since the Mexican War in 1848.

On arriving at Boquillas and just before crossing the river, Langhorne ordered the civilian newspapermen to remain behind. At approximately the same time, the supply truck broke down, and the newsmen offered to transport supplies in their own automobiles. Langhorne, manifestly upset at this turn of events, eventually consented. The backseats of each of the sedans were loaded with hundreds of pounds of gear and supplies.

After crossing the Rio Grande on May 8—a violation of agreed upon territorial restrictions imposed by the international border—the column had traveled only a mile into the Mexican state of Coahuila when a note was delivered to Langhorne from the bandits. It had been written by Jesse Deemer. Deemer stated that he and Payne were being treated well by their captors and were held at El Piño. He said the bandits offered to release him and Payne in exchange for Alvarez and the three others who were captured by the mineworkers. Langhorne was informed that the tiny village of El Piño was fifteen miles away to the south. Convinced that the bandits were unaware of the military pursuit, Langhorne decided to attack. In truth, El Piño was closer to fifty straight-line miles away, but the winding roads over the difficult terrain made the actual distance closer to one hundred true miles.

In spite of the extremely arduous and unmaintained roads that were more suitable to horses and oxcarts, Langhorne opted for a vehicular assault on El Piño. Each vehicle was loaded with Army sharpshooters, twenty-two in all. Langhorne, with no experience in this rugged desert mountain country of Coahuila, badly underestimated the landscape with all of its obstacles. With the major's Cadillac in the lead, the caravan set out, the cars bouncing and clanging along the nearly impossible road. Sections of deep and loose sand caused the vehicles to become stuck. The road was often choked with brush that had to be cut away to make room for the motorcars. When Langhorne realized they were making only four to five miles per hour, he opted to halt the caravan and await the mounted cavalry he knew to be following. By the time the horsemen came upon the parked cars, it was late in the day and time to set up camp.

Early the next morning, troopers were mounted and ready and set out for El Piño. Within the first mile or two, they realized they did not have enough water for the horses. While the men carried canteens, no provisions had been made for the mounts. It was assumed they would cross water-filled streams along the route, but this was not to be. Now and again they found some water in seep holes. This water would be quickly consumed by the first horses in line, then the rest would have to wait while the hole slowly refilled from the seepage.

After arriving at El Piño, some of the bandits wanted to execute Deemer. Before doing so, they sent Monroe Payne away on an errand so he would not be a witness. Suspicious, Payne returned just as Deemer was stood up against a wall and the bandits were readying their weapons and nerve. Payne stepped over and stood as close as possible to Deemer. When the Mexicans waved him away, he refused to leave Deemer's side. Even Deemer tried to get Payne to step away, but the black man remained by the side of his friend and employer.

At this point, one of the bandits argued to spare Deemer's life, claiming the storekeeper had long been a friend to the border Mexican families. Finally, the Mexicans put their weapons away.

It soon became clear to Langhorne that El Piño was a lot farther away than the informant stated. Following one of their seep hole breaks, the soldiers mounted up and rode twenty-two hours straight, rested for four, then were off again. At 4:00 a.m. the next morning, they arrived at El Piño and surrounded the village only to discover the bandits had fled. Langhorne ordered a search of every dwelling in the town. In one of them, the soldiers found Deemer and Payne, unharmed and visiting with the residents who were old friends of the storekeeper. On seeing the troopers, Deemer's first question was to ask about the news of World War I. Langhorne later released a statement to the press that the army had liberated Deemer and Payne, a gross overstatement designed to make Langhorne look good in the eyes of his superiors.

The cavalrymen set up camp just outside of El Piño. That evening, Langhorne invited Deemer to join him for dinner, but to his surprise, the storekeeper turned him down, opting instead to dine with one of the village's families. Langhorne and the other officers were stunned, and relations between Deemer and the major were strained from that point on.

While the cavalrymen were encamped at El Piño, they received word that the bandits were not far away in Rosita, about fifteen miles farther down the road. Langhorne, anxious to catch up to the malefactors, organized another vehicular assault, leading the way in his Cadillac that was operated by an enlisted man and followed by two of the automobiles owned by the newspapermen and filled with sharpshooters.

On entering Rosita, Langhorne spotted several men running out of a dwelling and fleeing into the nearby brush. Assuming they were guilty of something, Langhorne followed but was soon stopped by the thick vegetation that impeded passage of the automobiles.

Another man dashed out of an adobe, leaped upon a horse, and rode away. Believing the man to be one of the raiders, Langhorne set off in pursuit in his car. With the driver tearing through the brush and across arroyos and washes, Langhorne fired his pistol at the fleeing man, his target pointed out along the way by his driver. Langhorne's shots were wide of the mark and the outlaw escaped.

Less than a minute later, Langhorne encountered several men on horseback and ordered his driver to steer toward them. Langhorne opened fire as they advanced. The riders split up and Langhorne followed two of them, his Cadillac bouncing and jouncing along the rugged desert landscape. Intent on keeping their quarry in sight, the driver's attention was distracted. Unaware of the steep bank of an arroyo just ahead, the driver drove the Cadillac over it and plunged to the bottom where it became mired in deep sand. The fleeing bandits got away unscathed.

Langhorne decided to use El Piño as a base camp and conduct his pursuit from there. He ordered two detachments of cavalry deeper into Coahuila under the leadership of Captain Rhea. The soldiers rode seventy-five miles out and returned later with a number of the horses that had been stolen at Glenn Spring. During the foray deep into Mexico, the troop encountered a number of Mexicans who may or may not have been associated with the Glenn Spring and Boquillas attacks. Without bothering to question the men, Rhea surrounded them and fired into their midst, killing every one of them.

A second group of eight cavalrymen under the command of Lieutenant Stuart W. Cramer had also ranged farther to the south to the village of Castollón, part of the Castollón Ranch. Castollón was another twenty-five miles southwest of El Piño. As they made plans to set up night camp at a place called Santa Anita Well, some of the troopers climbed a nearby ridge and looked down the other side upon a group of heavily armed men, a number of horses, and an ox cart. Somehow, Cramer determined that these men had been participants in the raid at Boquillas and Glenn Spring.

Just after sundown, the troopers, who had gathered at the crest of the ridge, fired down into the bandit camp, killing one of them. They rushed down the slope toward their quarry, killing two more in the process. The remainder of the bandits escaped on horseback, leaving behind a collection of stolen goods. Cramer's men recovered seventeen horses and mules, nine rifles, several saddles, bridles, packs, and a great deal of stolen goods from Deemer's store, including overalls, hats, denims, dresses, shoes, and tools. Rhea took two prisoners—one of them an old man who was wounded during the exchange of gunfire and was likely not associated with the raiders at all. The other prisoner had a total of seven bullet wounds. The troopers returned to the base camp at El Piño.

Impressed by the reported successes of his troops, Langhorne wanted to continue on into Mexico to seek opportunities to acquire more glory for himself and his command. Unfortunately for his plans, however, he received orders from Washington, DC, to return to Texas immediately as military intelligence had detected an elite fighting force of some fifteen hundred Yaqui Indian troops on their way to his location to attack his soldiers. One hundred and seventy-five miles later, Langhorne and his entire command crossed back into Texas at Boquillas.

Langhorne's sixteen-day incursion into Mexico was reported a success: Hostages were rescued, a significant amount of stolen goods and livestock recovered, and bandits killed or captured. Not a single American was killed. In all, they traveled just over 550 miles. Langhorne's punitive expedition into Mexico proved to be far more successful than General Pershing's quest to capture or kill Pancho Villa following the Columbus Raid. Neither Pershing, nor any of his soldiers, ever saw Villa.

Though claiming success, Langhorne's expedition into Mexico was, according to author Gomez, "insufficient to bring an end to the bandit raiding." If anything, raids increased, and while retaliation from the military, the Texas Rangers, vigilantes, and others were employed, these forces, formal and informal, were by and large inefficient to prevent the across-the-border raids.

Following the conclusion of World War I in 1918, Major General Charles T. Menhor, chief of the Army Air Service, realizing the prevailing border security methods were not working and that something more efficient and effective needed to be employed, ordered the establishment of an aerial border patrol on June 16, 1919. A total of eighteen aircraft from Ellington Field in Houston and Kelly Fields in San Antonio arrived at Fort Bliss, Texas, to form the Eleventh Aero Squadron. Some of the pilots received instruction to fly reconnaissance missions along the border from El Paso to Presidio. The rest of the pilots, operating out of Marfa, were to patrol the border in the Big Bend area from the canyon country to Sanderson, Texas. For two years, the twelve-cylinder DeHavilland-4 fighter aircraft, each armed with two .30 caliber machine guns, served as an important contribution to the ground-based US Cavalry activities in the Big Bend region.

On April 1, 1920, the War Department issued General Order No. 5, which reduced the defense forces along the Texas-Mexico border, limiting it to only a few strategically placed locations manned by smaller detachments. Around the same time, Mexican president and general Alvaro Obregon increased the number of Mexican troops deployed along the border in an effort to reduce banditry. In 1921, the US Eleventh Aero Squadron was recalled and eventually disbanded.

CHAPTER TWELVE

The San Ignacio and San Benito Raids

To STATE THAT THERE WAS UNREST ALONG THE BORDER BETWEEN THE United States and Mexico during the first two decades of the twentieth century would be an understatement. Americans remained nervous at the goings-on south of the border as a result of the Mexican Revolution, and were concerned that some of the unpleasantness might spill over into Texas. When they learned about the Plan of San Diego, it created even more reason for concern. Mexicans calling themselves Seditionists were dedicated to bringing American border states under the control of Mexico and then-president Venustiano Carranza. In an attempt to accomplish this, a number of attacks were launched on isolated military outposts as well as small towns and ranches, all within striking distance of the border.

The Seditionists were originally led by a man named Luis de la Rosa, but within a short time he was arrested by Carranza agents. Around the same time, other Seditionist leaders were also arrested on a variety of charges. The arrests effectively put an end to the planned raids into Texas, at least for a time.

A man named Esteban Fierros, a superintendent of the Mexican National Railway, decided to step in and take charge of the border campaign after de la Rosa was rendered ineffective. As Fierros pondered strategies, a contingent of US cavalrymen pursued a band of raiding Mexicans across the border and into Matamoros. This was all the incentive Fierros needed. He organized a plan to attack the small Texas town of San Ignacio on June 15, 1916.

San Ignacio was a tiny village on the Texas side of the Rio Grande some thirty miles downriver from Laredo and 180 miles northwest of Brownsville. The population was less than two hundred, but in the village could be found a post office, three general stores including a drugstore, and a number of dwellings. In response to the growing border unrest in this part of Texas, soldiers from Troops I and M of the Fourteenth Cavalry were stationed at a camp located a short distance from San Ignacio, a total of 150 men.

With no warning whatsoever, the cavalry camp was attacked by approximately one hundred Mexicans. It was reported that a sentry heard some unusual noises in the brush a short distance from the camp and alerted his commanding officer. Several minutes later, a patrol was sent out to investigate and was immediately fired upon. The Americans retreated and stationed themselves in a series of trenches to defend themselves against the invaders. Military documents reveal that three enlisted men were killed and six wounded. One of the wounded would die the following day.

Although the several accounts of the battle differed, the consensus is that the Americans killed between six and eight raiders. Six bodies were found, but reports stated that it was apparent that other bodies had been dragged from the site. A half-dozen Mexicans were captured.

One of the Mexican bodies was identified as Lieutenant-Colonel Villareal, an officer in the Constitutional Army. The Americans concluded that Villareal was a Seditionist and according to some, likely a Villista. One of the captured Mexicans, however, insisted that Villareal was a Carranzista officer who was simply following orders. The US military did not accept this explanation.

The commander of the American forces at San Ignacio was Major Alonzo Gray. Following the raid, Gray was authorized to lead a punitive expedition into Mexico to pursue and punish the raiders. Gray led his troops into the Mexican state of Tamaulipas on June 16. Once across the border, however, he was unable to find the trail of the raiders and returned unsuccessful.

While Gray was in Mexico, another group of raiders, estimated to number thirty, attacked the military encampment at San Benito, Texas, located only twenty miles from Brownsville. General James Parker, commander of the 26th Infantry, responded by placing Colonel Robert Bullard in charge of four hundred soldiers and sending them into Mexico in pursuit of the fleeing raiders. After traveling only a short distance from the Rio Grande, Bullard's soldiers engaged their quarry in a skirmish. Though hundreds of shots were fired, there were no casualties on either side. Coming to the aid of Bullard's forces was a squadron of Third Cavalry soldiers led by Major Edward Anderson. Anderson's troops arrived just as the fighting slackened.

Learning of the US Army crossing into Mexico, President Carranza ordered General Alfredo Ricault to assemble one thousand soldiers in Matamoros and attack the Americans, forcing them back into Texas. Ricault's troopers captured around forty US soldiers. Following this, they attacked Anderson's force as it fled back toward the Rio Grande. During the running firefight, two Mexicans were killed but none of the Americans were struck.

Events along the Texas-Mexico border settled down for a period of time, but the worst was yet to come.

CHAPTER THIRTEEN

The Brite Ranch Raid

THE CATTLE AND SHEEP RANCH OF LUCAS CHARLES BRITE IN WESTERN Presidio County, Texas, was nestled in a scenic location in the eastern foothills of the Sierra Vieja and Candelaria Rim and at the foot of Capote Peak. In addition to raising livestock, Lucas Brite operated a store that supplied canned goods and other foodstuffs, hardware, tools, auto supplies, and tobacco, as well as some articles of clothing, to area residents, some sixty in number. He also carried guns and ammunition.

Brite, originally from Frio County, Texas, saw promise in the abundant and rich grasslands. He envisioned raising large, strong, and healthy herds of cattle on this graze located thirty miles west of Marfa and ten miles from the Mexican border. In all, Brite acquired 125,000 acres, an area larger than the state of Rhode Island.

Brite stocked his ranch with Hereford cattle. In 1904, he registered the Bar Cross brand and in a short time was widely recognized as an intelligent and hardworking rancher. He was eventually elected to prominent positions in a number of livestock organizations. In addition to growing influential, Brite became wealthy. In 1911 he wrote a check for twenty-five thousand dollars to Texas Christian University to endow the Brite College of the Bible.

On Christmas Day, 1917, the Brite family was gathered at their home in Marfa, thirty miles to the east. Most of Brite's ranch hands were given time off for the holidays. The ranch was left in the care of foreman T. T. Van Neill. Keeping Neill company was his father, Sam H. Neill, a

Lucas Brite

US Customs inspector in the Big Bend region. In addition to both Neills and their families, the ranch house was to host Christmas dinner guests who would arrive from Marfa and Valentine.

Unknown to Neill, a contingent of forty-five Mexicans was riding toward the ranch during the pre-dawn hours, keeping out of sight by traveling along the deep arroyos and washes. Along the way, they spotted telephone lines and cut them.

Some writers have claimed that the party of Mexicans represented a force of Pancho Villa's soldiers and/or supporters, and that their mission was to procure guns and ammunition, as well as supplies and provisions. Others maintain the raiders were Carranzistas. The commander of the

Big Bend military district insisted he was in possession of information that the raiders were Villistas but were impersonating Carranzistas. Some assert that one of the raiders was Placido Villanueva, who once served as a colonel in Pancho Villa's army. There are some who insist that Villa himself was behind the raid, but evidence is scanty to nonexistent. Still others maintain the raid was orchestrated by notorious border bandit Chico Cano. The possibility remains that the raiders likely represented no one but themselves, and amounted to no more than bandits out on a raid.

During this time, and particularly in this part of Texas, ranchers and their families and ranch hands were often at the mercy of bandits and raiders. Raids were commonplace, and in their looting the raiders were indiscriminate, killing both Texans and Mexicans. The raiding parties were made up of former Villistas, deserters, and professional outlaws. Their objectives were mainly to steal cattle and horses along with weapons and foodstuffs. Having completed a raid, they would dash back across the river into Mexico, often hiding out in the homes of villagers residing along the border.

Sam Neill rose early and made a pot of coffee. He decided to build up the fires in the house's two fireplaces but the kindling basket was empty. Taking the container, he walked outside to the woodpile, filled it with sticks, and returned to the house. After getting one fire started, he returned to the woodpile for another load, which he carried back inside. Once the fires were going well, Neill sat down in the kitchen with the cook, Crescencia Natividad, and enjoyed coffee and conversation when he spotted six riders approaching fast and up the road toward the house. When Neill saw the riders pull revolvers from their holsters, he decided to wake his son.

The newcomers dismounted, took cover, and began firing their weapons at the house. After shouting an alarm, the elder Neill grabbed a rifle and a revolver, dashed outside, and after taking cover near a corner of the ranch house, began returning fire. Moments later, the rest of the raiders arrived, surrounded the house, and began shooting amid cries of *"Mueran los gringos!"* Death to the Americans.

During the gun battle, Sam Neill was wounded in the leg and suffered a flesh wound on his nose. Though bleeding and in some pain, he held his ground. His son and other family members were shooting from windows. At one point Sam spotted a rider dressed in an officer's uniform of the Carranzista army riding toward the house. Neill assumed this man was the leader, so he shot him off his horse, killing him. During the gunfight, four of the raiders were wounded. The officer and wounded men were carried away by their fellows.

The raiders captured two workers who had remained at the ranch for the holiday. They instructed one of them, José Sanchez (some accounts say Tomás Sanchez), to go to ranch foreman Neill and tell him that if they did not surrender, the other ranch hand would be killed. They also demanded the keys to the store. The Neills declined to surrender and informed the raiders that the keys were in the possession of a neighbor, Pierre Guyon, who lived several hundred yards away. Guyon was the manager of the store. Sanchez was sent to the Guyon residence, obtained the keys, and handed them over to the raiders.

Once inside the store, the raiders helped themselves to clothing, hats, ammunition, cloth, tools, shoes, and tobacco. What they did not take they dumped onto the floor. Forty dollars was taken from the cash register. They found a safe but were unable to break into it. Brite later stated that the safe contained a significant amount of money. Most of the bandits changed their trail-worn clothes for the new ones, and left the store wearing better clothes than they ever had in their lives. In all, it was estimated the raiders took about fifteen hundred dollars worth of goods. Several others went to the nearby barn and took all of the saddles and tack they could find. They also rounded up twenty saddle horses.

While many of the raiders were in the store, postman Mickey Welch drove his mail wagon pulled by two mules into the yard and up to the store that also served as a post office for the region. The Brite Ranch was a regular stop on his Candelaria-to-Valentine run. Welch had two passengers. One account states that one of the passengers was a clock repairman and the other was a Carranzista soldier who was fleeing the Mexican Revolution following a recent defeat by Villa's forces at Ojinaga. Another account describes the passengers as Demetrio Holguin, a mining engineer, and another Mexican national named Ernesto Juarez.

Before coming to a stop, Welch's vehicle was fired on by the raiders, and the two passengers were killed. Welch was taken prisoner. He was ordered to unhitch the mules and then return to his seat in the wagon from which he loudly cursed his captors.

In an odd move, the raiders told Welch he was free to go and pointed him in the direction of Guyon's residence in the distance. After walking a few dozen yards, the irritated Welch turned around and made an attempt to retrieve his mules. Two of the raiders caught him in the act, beat him, and then dragged him into a back room of the store where they hung him from one of the rafters. As the mailman struggled and kicked while straining against the noose, a raider named Jesús "Pegleg" Renteria stepped up and slit his throat, wiped his blade on the dead man's shirt, and then cut him down. In addition to missing a leg, Renteria lost part of an arm and had a hook attached. Another of his nicknames was "El Gancho," which means "The Hook."

Foreman Neill was worried: His small force was outnumbered ten-to-one and he dreaded continuing a firefight with the raiders. The gunfire had died down somewhat while the raiders were preoccupied with looting the store, but Neill was concerned they would not leave before killing everyone.

While trying to decide what to do, Neill watched while the bandits loaded their stolen goods onto their horses. A short time later, one set of Christmas dinner guests arrived. The Reverend H. M. Bandy drove his car into the yard and up to the house, completely unaware that a raid was going on. Bandy was the pastor of the First Christian Church in Marfa.

As Bandy, his wife, and two other women were exiting the automobile, they were surrounded by the raiders, revolvers aimed at the newcomers. When it appeared as though they intended to kill the Bandys, foreman Neill sent out a young Mexican houseboy to explain to the raider that Bandy was a *padre*, a cleric. The raiders allowed Bandy and his party to enter the house.

Once inside, Bandy sized up the situation immediately. He directed his attention to Sam Neill, who was bleeding badly from his wounded nose and suffering severe pain from the leg wound. Sam begged for a shot of whiskey, and as Bandy's wife poured it for him, the preacher picked up a weapon and prepared to assist in defending the house.

Around this time, Hodge Hunter, accompanied by his wife, pulled his car up to the Guyon House. Hunter was a Valentine businessman and brother-in-law to Van Neill. They were on their way to have Christmas with the Neills when they stopped to greet the neighbor. They were unaware of the raid until Guyon called a warning from his doorway. Hunter spotted several of the raiders. He turned his car around and sped back to Valentine for help.

When the gunfire had erupted earlier, another of Brite's neighbors, James Cobb, heard it and, concerned, made his way over toward the origin of the sound. Keeping out of sight, Cobb arrived as the looters were carrying goods from the store. Deducing what was taking place, he ran back to his residence and telephoned Brite in Marfa and informed him of what was going on. Brite, in turn, called Colonel George Langhorne of the Eighth Cavalry for help.

With the successful looting accomplished, the raiders appeared to lose interest in Neill and the others in the house. Instead of departing, the bandits chose to remain in the area and rest. Around 12:30 p.m., they began to gather up more of the stolen loot and load it onto their horses. Herding Brite's saddle stock before them, they departed the ranch, crossed the Candelaria Rim, and headed for Los Fresnos, a small town across the Rio Grande a few miles to the southwest. Los Fresnos Ford was a popular crossing place for rustlers.

As the US cavalry troops stationed at Fort D. A. Russell were in the middle of a specially prepared Christmas noon meal, word of the raid on the Brite Ranch arrived. Without hesitation, the soldiers loaded into trucks and cars, a few rode horseback, and all set out for the ranch thirty miles away. In all, there were one hundred troopers. At about the same time, Presidio County sheriff Ira Cline assembled a posse and, filling three automobiles, headed for the Brite Ranch. These were joined by a contingent of Texas Rangers captained by J. M. Fox.

At border locations such as Candelaria, Holland, and Evetts Ranch, outposts of the Eighth Cavalry were contacted by telephone and informed of the situation. These troopers were ordered to head for the known border crossings into Mexico to head off the raiders.

From the time of the initial alert, it took the cavalrymen and county lawmen an hour to get to the Brite Ranch. Among them was Grover Webb, a US Customs inspector who was intimately familiar with this section of the Big Bend country. As the first of the vehicles arrived at the ranch, Webb spotted the raiders fleeing along the crest of the Sierra Vieja Mountains three miles away. Along the path of their flight, they discarded some of the items burgled from the store, along with the bodies of their dead. The rugged path taken by the raiders, as well as the steep grade of the mountain range, inhibited pursuit by automobile. Since all of Brite's saddle horses were taken by the raiders, those who arrived by vehicle had no opportunity to continue pursuit. Langhorne sent some of his troopers around to the nearby ranches to conscript horses to aid in the chase.

A bit later, the mounted troopers from Marfa arrived and continued the chase. By this time the bandits were descending the southwestern slope of the Sierra Vieja and were out of sight. Along this portion of the route, they discarded more of the loot in an attempt to lighten their load and facilitate their escape.

On the morning of December 25, the raiders crossed the river into Mexico at Los Fresnos Ford. Later that day, a total of two hundred members of Troops M and G of the Eighth Cavalry arrived at the ford, crossed it, and pursued the bandits into Mexico, following a trail that roughly paralleled the Rio Grande toward the Mexican town of Pilares.

The next day and after several miles of riding along this trail, the American forces caught up with fifteen of the raiders and engaged them in a running gun battle. Ten of the bandits were killed in a canyon in the Sierra Pilares range not far from Pilares, Mexico. The remaining five escaped into the mountains. Only one soldier, John F. Kelly, was struck, and he suffered a non-fatal wound.

The soldiers recovered some of the stolen goods. Most of the horses and mules were lost during the chase, but a number of them were rounded up. Several of those that were found were in such poor condition that they had to be shot. That evening, the cavalry, in possession of much of Brite's stolen property, crossed the river back into the United States.

As news of the Brite Ranch raid spread throughout the county, residents feared that more raids could occur, and a mild panic swept the region. Citizens took up arms and established patrols around the towns and ranches and along the roads, ever on the lookout for Mexican raiders. Most were convinced that the border bandit Chico Cano led and/ or took part in the Brite Ranch raid, but this has never been verified. Because of Cano's prominence as an outlaw and the scourge of Texas ranchers, he was, guilty or not, blamed for nearly every depredation that took place along the border. In Marfa, women and children were escorted to the courthouse for safety, around which stood armed guards.

On December 29, the Stockman's Club of Marfa hosted a meeting of some two hundred cattle ranchers, Texas Rangers, and citizens. Texas Ranger Jim Gillette and Lieutenant-Colonel Langhorne addressed the gathering and called for aggressive action regarding raids on Texas soil. A decision was made to organize a vigilante committee whose responsibility would be to register the Mexican populations of Brewster, Culberson, Jeff Davis, Hudspeth, and Presidio Counties. In addition, any arms possessed by the Mexicans were to be confiscated. A telegram was sent to the Texas adjutant general requesting official status for the vigilante group.

It can be argued that the fear and paranoia of the residents of this border region led to the formation of the vigilante committee, along with some general dislike and distrust of any non-Anglos. In the end, the activities of the committee proved to be worthless and a waste of time. It has been judged that all of the Brite Ranch raiders were from Mexico, not Texas. The responsibilities of the committee did not extend across the Rio Grande.

Many of the area residents believed the existence of the vigilante committee, as well as the attack on Pilares, would serve to discourage further incursions of bandits into the United States. It was not to be, for a scant three months later, it would happen again.

Chapter Fourteen

Revenge at Porvenir

PORVENIR WAS A TINY RANCHING AND FARMING COMMUNITY IN NORTH-west Presidio County, Texas, located near the banks of the Rio Grande a short distance upstream from the Mexican town of Pilares. According to unreliable census data, the population of Porvenir consisted of 140 Mexicans and one or two Anglos. Most were involved with raising crops along the floodplain of the river as well as tending small herds of goats, cattle, and a few horses. It was, for the most part, a subsistence living. A significant percentage of the Porvenir citizens arrived at the town in 1910 to escape from the ongoing civil war that ravaged the countryside of Chihuahua. *Porvenir* is a Spanish word for future, and for many who lived here, that is precisely what it represented. They had no inkling of the disaster that was about to befall the town.

Porvenir had a small school, a blacksmith shop, and little else. If the citizens were in need of a post office or a store, they traveled to the Brite Ranch, a two-day round trip on horseback through rugged country across the Sierra Vieja and back. As a result of conducting business, many of the citizens of Porvenir knew the Brites and their store manager, Pierre Guyon. Relationships were cordial and neighborly.

Following the raid on the Brite Ranch on Christmas Day, 1917, US military and Texas state officials pondered an appropriate response above and beyond the pursuit into Mexico by the US cavalry troops and hastily formed a posse. It was concluded that greater border security was necessary, but the US military was unable to provide it as a result of their attention being diverted by the needs of World War I. The responsibility fell upon Texas officials.

A state guard was formed, and before long consisted of two cavalry brigades and one infantry brigade, a total of fifteen thousand men. The Texas State Legislature appropriated sufficient money for an expanded Texas Ranger force. In addition, a volunteer branch of the Texas Rangers was established. It was named the Loyalty Rangers and described as a "secret service" arm of the Texas Rangers. Their primary duties involved investigating reports of rustling, draft evasion, desertion, and anti-American activities. Further, another organized group called the Special Rangers assisted where necessary. This latter group was made up mostly of cattlemen with ranches located along and near the Rio Grande.

Literature of the American West is replete with tales of the heroism and derring-do of the Texas Rangers, of how these men served to protect settlers and citizens from the threat of Indians and other menace. One of the earliest and chief apologists for the Texas Rangers was the noted Texas writer Walter Prescott Webb, whose book *The Texas Rangers* portrayed this unique law enforcement organization as being composed of self-sacrificing men who were devoted to the law and were to be valued, honored, and revered. Subsequent books and articles, in large part based on Webb's book, perpetuated this image. During the ensuing years, Hollywood likewise portrayed Texas Rangers as a kind of frontier superhero group. Nothing could be further from the truth.

While there is no doubt that many Texas Rangers were dedicated to service and an honest application of the law, the ultimate truth is that many, if not most, of them were drifters, riffraff, and thugs. Many Rangers were former outlaws. Being a Texas Ranger along the US–Mexico border was the nearest thing to having a license to kill.

Captain J. M. Fox was the commander of Ranger Company B based in Marfa, which consisted only of Fox and eleven Ranger privates. With these few men, most of them inexperienced, Fox was given the responsibility of patrolling and protecting four thousand square miles of land along the Mexican border. Fox also had at his disposal some two hundred volunteers, mostly cattlemen. The majority of them were informal members of the Ranger force with no official appointment.

As a result of the lobbying from a number of cattlemen, Fox grew convinced that Porvenir was a haven for bandits and raiders, and that it should be targeted. Much of this response grew out of overt racism that dominated the feelings of many of the cattlemen. Anger at the Brite Ranch raid had not yet diffused, and the killings of Mickey Welch, Jack Howard, and two Rangers aggravated the wound. In addition, a number of the cattlemen regarded the Mexicans who lived on the Texas side of the border as little more than squatters who survived by raiding, thieving, and killing. Likely closer to the truth was that the cattlemen resented the Mexicans living on what they insisted should be regarded as open rangeland.

The idea has also been advanced that the incursion into Porvenir was stimulated by a rancher named Tom Snider. It was suggested by a Porvenir schoolteacher named Warren that Snider had sold stolen horses to some of the Mexicans at Porvenir and told the Texas Rangers that several of the bandits who raided the Brite Ranch lived in the village. He encouraged the Rangers to invade the town in order that his crime would not be reported. While provocative, no evidence has ever surfaced to support this theory.

Near the end of January 1918, Fox ordered a contingent of Company B Rangers led by Ranger Bud Weaver to Porvenir. On January 23, a group of Rangers rode in an automobile to the John Poole Ranch at the Candelaria Rim where they obtained horses to cross over the rim and head for Porvenir. At the Poole Ranch, they were joined by several other volunteers, all cattlemen. In all, they numbered forty. Mounted, armed, and vengeance-minded, the force rode down the rim and toward Porvenir. They arrived shortly after midnight on January 24 and surrounded the town.

In an odd move, a number of the Rangers donned masks. At 1:00 a.m., they roused the sleeping Mexicans and ordered them out of their dwellings. After the residents were herded into a group where they were held at gunpoint, several Rangers searched through the adobes and jacales for weapons. In all, they seized two rifles, a shotgun, and a pistol.

With the search completed, the Rangers released the townsfolk save for Eutimio Gonzalez, Manuel Fierro, and Ramon Nieves. The three were questioned about their shoes—each wore a brand of shoe—Hamilton Brown—that was only available in the region at the Brite Store. Several Hamilton Brown shoes had been stolen during the Christmas day raid.

On departing Porvenir, the Rangers took Gonzalez, Fierro, and Nieves with them. Several miles later they set up camp in an abandoned railroad tunnel not far from a coal mine. Here, the three Mexicans were questioned further about the Brite Ranch raid. Since none of the men knew anything about it, they were subsequently released. Nieves and Gonzales walked back to Porvenir while Fierro decided to return to Mexico.

Unsatisfied with the outcome of the midnight raid on Porvenir, the Rangers began making plans for another. They rode to Camp Evetts, an Eighth Cavalry posting a short distance from Porvenir, arriving on the afternoon of January 27. The troopers assigned to Camp Evetts, Troop G, had experienced only positive relations with the residents of Porvenir and never regarded them as a threat to anyone.

The Rangers were not welcome at the camp as a result of previous frictions between them and the soldiers. A number of incidents had been reported wherein Rangers arrested soldiers for some imagined infraction or another, levied a fine to be paid in cash on the spot, and then pocketed the money.

When the Rangers arrived, they sought post commander Captain Henry H. Anderson. After locating his tent, they presented him with a letter from Colonel George T. Langhorne, Anderson's commanding officer. The letter ordered Anderson to provide military assistance to the Rangers relative to going to Porvenir and "subduing the village." Anderson, knowing well that the residents of Porvenir were innocent of anything having to do with the Brite Ranch raid, was unnerved by the order and placed a call to Langhorne to verify the letter. Langhorne confirmed it, and Anderson sent word to his men to "prepare for the mission to Porvenir." According to researcher Glenn Justice, Anderson instructed them to "surround the village, see that no one escaped, and seize all firearms and weapons."

The Rangers, supported by twelve cavalrymen of Troop G (one report mentions forty) and led by Anderson, departed Camp Evetts for Porvenir at 10:30 p.m. The hostility that existed between the Rangers and the troopers was palpable during the ride. The two groups rode separately and there was little mixing. Each Ranger carried a pair of Colt .45 revolvers along with crossed bandoliers filled with cartridges. According to reports, the Rangers appeared anxious and jittery. During the ride they bolstered their courage with periodic drinks of whiskey. Several became noticeably drunk.

For the second time in only a few days, the little town of Porvenir was surrounded at midnight. The troopers rode through the village awakening the sleeping residents and forcing them out into the bitterly cold night. As the Porvenirans built a fire to try to keep warm, the troopers assured them that they were only looking for bandits and that when the search was completed they could return to their houses. Once again, their dwellings were searched. Only one very old and likely inoperative handgun was found along with a few knives. Not a single item of stolen Brite Store property was found. While the soldiers searched the dwellings, the Rangers sat on their horses apart from the main body of soldiers.

The residents, huddled around the fire, appeared nervous. Relations between them and the hated Rangers were never good. Accounts of unprovoked Ranger attacks on Mexican villages and travelers ranged up and down the Rio Grande Valley. The Rangers were known to shoot and kill Mexicans for no reason at all.

When the troopers had completed their search, one of the Rangers came forward and asked Anderson to withdraw his troops. The Ranger explained that they wanted to question the Porvenirans in Spanish, a language none of the soldiers knew. Anderson agreed to the request, but reminded the Ranger that he was acquainted with every Mexican in the village and assured him that none of the bandits associated with the Brite Ranch raid were among them. With that, Anderson ordered his men to a location a short distance away to wait for the Rangers to complete their interrogation.

Once the troopers were out of sight, the Rangers separated the men from the women and children. Of the group of men, the Rangers picked fifteen between sixteen and seventy-two years of age and, at gunpoint, herded them out of the light of the fire and toward a bluff a short distance away. Unsettled and having a bad feeling about what was to happen, the women and children broke down in sobs. Moments later, the fifteen Mexicans were executed, shot down at close range by the drunken Texas Rangers.

Following the killings, the Rangers raced back to where their horses were tethered, mounted up, and rode through the village telling the women that they would return to kill them all. This done, they galloped away "shouting drunken, Comanche-like yells." Anderson, disturbed and appalled at what he heard and suspected, led his men back into the village where he watched the women crying and mourning over their dead relatives.

Leaving a small contingent of troopers in the village to guard against the return of the Rangers, Anderson sent word to the nearest priest in Candelaria, and then led the rest of the men back to Camp Evetts. By dawn of the following day, Porvenir was deserted save for the few soldiers ordered to remain. The Mexicans gathered what they could carry and fled across the river to Pilares.

According to writer Glenn Justice, the Mexicans killed by the Rangers were for the most part "poor tenant farmers with large families" and forty-two children were orphaned that night. It was subsequently and formally determined that not a single one of the Porvenirans had been associated with the Brite Ranch raid. The mass executions were motivated by nothing more than hate and misplaced revenge.

News of what was called the "Porvenir Massacre" ranged throughout this portion of the Texas Big Bend region. The Mexican residents of the village of Candelaria, located eighteen miles downriver and on the

Texas side, feared an imminent attack by the Rangers. Most of them gathered their families and, in their panic, fled across the border to the town of Barrancos, leaving behind all of their belongings including their livestock.

During the morning following the killings, an aged Mexican woman walked across the shallow Rio Grande back into Porvenir and asked the troopers remaining there if they would help her load the bodies of the slain men onto a cart so that she might return them to Mexico to be buried. The soldiers assisted her and then watched her re-cross the river in the cart, headed toward the graveyard in Pilares. Within a week, a small contingent of soldiers from Camp Evetts arrived at Pilares and proceeded to burn down the abandoned dwellings.

To his discredit, Captain Anderson lied about the incident at Porvenir, reporting that one of his patrols discovered the bodies of the fifteen dead men on the morning of January 29 and could make no determination relative to how they had been killed. It is evident that if the truth came out regarding Anderson's carelessness relative to protecting the citizens of Porvenir and allowing the Texas Rangers to slay fifteen unarmed men, that punishment would follow. It was a cover-up, plain and simple. And it was easy to get away with, since the bodies had been buried in Mexico and there was no evidence to suggest anything that could prove to be embarrassing to the US Army. In subsequent interviews, Anderson denied any knowledge of the killings.

Henry Warren, the schoolmaster at Porvenir, lived a mile from the village and learned about the killings the following dawn. He rode to the town and observed the results of the massacre. Warren felt an obligation to inform the country of what had occurred at Porvenir. During the following weeks he sent releases to a variety of newspapers, but his version of what happened was contradicted by Anderson and Colonel Langhorne. Langhorne insisted that the US Army had no knowledge of what happened at Porvenir and warned Warren to tone down his complaints.

Warren decided legal action was necessary and attempted to submit his case to the United States Court of Claims. He got nowhere. Because he now had no school in which to teach at Porvenir, Warren went to

Candelaria where he sought employment. The US military was determined to make life hard for Warren. He was described by Lieutenant Leonard F. Matlack as "a dangerous man in that he agitates among the Mexicans on both sides of the river and keeps the situation at a boiling point." With pressure from the Army, Warren's application to teach in the Candelaria district was rejected. He was subsequently removed from the town.

Not long after the Porvenir killings, an article written by Ranger captain J. M. Fox appeared in a number of newspapers throughout the country. Fox maintained that his Rangers had come under attack by the Porvenirans, shooting at the Rangers when they arrived in the town. The fifteen Mexicans were killed, claimed Fox, in self-defense when the Rangers returned gunfire. Fox further reported that the Rangers confiscated a number of items that had been stolen from the Brite Store during the raid. Fox, of course, was never present at Porvenir.

In response to Fox's version of the event, survivors of the Porvenir massacre submitted a challenge in a Mexican court of inquiry. The consensus was that the victims were innocent men who had been "brutally murdered by the Rangers." The results of the inquiry were sent to the Mexican ambassador in Washington, DC, and to Ranger W. M. Hanson, a captain in the Loyalty Ranger Force. Hanson appointed himself to investigate, but did nothing to clear up the matter.

As many of the specific horrible details of the Porvenir killings surfaced during the ensuing months, US Army special inspector Colonel W. J. Glascow examined the charges against the army and the Texas Rangers. He determined that the Rangers had been responsible for the killings and that they were led to Porvenir by Anderson and Troop G. The results of Glascow's investigation led Texas governor William P. Hobby to disband Ranger Company B and dismiss the Rangers who were involved in the incident. Ranger Captain Fox submitted his resignation, but subsequently claimed he had been fired for political reasons.

In January 1919, Brownsville, Texas, state representative J. T. Canales submitted to a joint committee of the Texas Senate and House concerned with the state Ranger force eighteen charges of Texas Ranger corruption and abuse of Mexican citizens of the United States, with the Porvenir incident being foremost among the examples. Charges against the Rangers included assault, torture of prisoners, drunkenness, and murder.

In testifying, Canales stated that the state Ranger force consisted of "men of desperate character, notoriously known as gunmen, their only qualification being that they can kill a man first and then investigate afterward," and that the Rangers are allowed by the adjutant general to "terrorize and intimidate the citizens of the state." In the aftermath of Canales's effort, the state Texas Ranger force was reorganized. No charges were ever filed against Captain Fox or any others of Company B.

Matters along the Texas border were far from settled. Reeling from the reign of terror inflicted by the Texas Rangers as well as the growing racism and hostility manifested by the region's Anglo ranchers, the massacre at Porvenir was still an open wound for many Mexicans, and reprisal was not long in coming.

Chapter Fifteen

The Neville Ranch Raid

If the Texas Rangers and the US Army thought that their actions at Porvenir would forever settle the real and imagined border problems, they were badly mistaken. In the Mexican town of Pilares across the Rio Grande from Porvenir, passions ran high and retaliation was on the minds of a number of the men, many of them relatives of the fifteen residents mercilessly slain by the Rangers at Porvenir. Two months after the horrible killings, they decided to take action. Their target was the Neville Ranch located in northern Presidio County.

Despite the occasional and ongoing border difficulties, fifty-year-old rancher Edwin Watts "Ed" Neville experienced few problems. His large ranch extended from a few miles upstream from Porvenir northwest-ward through Presidio County, into Jeff Davis County, and on into the southern part of Hudspeth County. While encompassing many acres, Neville's ranch was for the most part located in desert scrub country. He was therefore unable to maintain the large healthy herds found on the rich grasslands of the Brite Ranch.

When he learned of the Brite Ranch raid, Neville grew concerned that it could be the first of several that might occur along the border. He sent his wife and two daughters to the town of Van Horn twenty miles away. Neville, along with his nineteen-year-old son, Glen (some accounts spell the name Glenn) remained at the ranch house six miles from Porvenir. The ranch house was mostly constructed of logs, a two-room structure with a dogtrot between the rooms.

Neville worked hard to improve the land and productivity of his ranch. He constructed a series of stock tanks to trap surface water. He was also busy preparing fields for growing hay and vegetables and planning to irrigate them with the water he captured by his system of small reservoirs. As a result of this activity, Neville employed several Mexican laborers, most of them residents of Porvenir and Pilares who returned to their homes on weekends. Several of Neville's Porvenir workers likely escaped being murdered during the slaughter conducted by the Texas Rangers because they were working at the ranch at the time the massacre took place.

When Neville's workers learned of the killings at Porvenir, they informed their employer they were quitting, going to Mexico, and joining the revolutionary army of Pancho Villa. The men requested their wages. To pay off his men, Neville had to travel to Van Horn to withdraw the money from the bank. When the men were paid off, they thanked Neville and departed. Only one remained—Adrian Castillo, who lived on the ranch with his wife, Clara (some accounts record her name as Rosa), and three young sons. Clara was employed as a cook.

Two months following the Porvenir killings, Ed Neville was in Van Horn conducting business when he encountered a US Army cavalry patrol. Recognizing the rancher, the leader informed him of rumors relating to an impending raid on his ranch. After completing his business and stocking up on provisions and supplies, Neville sped back to the ranch house, arriving just before dark.

It was March 25, 1918. As Neville and his son were eating supper and discussing the news of a possible raid, they heard the sound of approaching riders. Neville rose from the table and went to the door. Peering outside into the dusk, he spotted what he claimed were fifty Mexican raiders, most on horseback and some on foot. They spotted Neville and immediately opened fire on the house. As the bullets easily pierced the smallish log walls of the house, Neville turned and ran for his rifle. He fired several shots at the raiders and was convinced he struck one of them. Realizing he was badly outnumbered, he dashed out the door intending to seek shelter in a wash three hundred yards away. As he ran he yelled for Glen and the Castillos to follow him.

Neville had a significant head start on his son, and by the time the young man exited the door of the house he was surrounded by the raiders. Glen had no sooner stepped outside when he was shot down, mortally wounded. Several of the raiders approached the suffering victim and beat him with rifle butts. When they tired of the assault, they entered the house with the intention of looting it.

Adrian Castillo, concerned about flying bullets, instructed his wife and children to lie down on the floor. Before she was able to do so, she was struck in the breast by a bullet. Believing the raiders would not harm his children, Adrian dashed out of the room and ran. The raiders fired after him but he managed to escape. He ran for a mile, then after spotting one of the ranch horses, he mounted up and rode to the nearest cavalry outpost to report the attack.

Neville made it to the wash where he hid for a time. After an anxious and fruitless wait for his son, he changed position, moving from one sheltered location to another until dawn. All the while, he could hear the raiders as they looted the house and barn. After rounding up nine horses and one mule belonging to Neville, they finally rode away at 3:30 a.m. At one point, Neville was close enough to the raiders to recognize one of them—Jesús Nieves, a native of the village of San Antonio in the Mexican state of Chihuahua.

It is possible that while Ed Neville lay in hiding, the ranch was subjected to a second raid by a different group of raiders. Author Elton Miles submits that a company of Villistas led by a man named Jesús Urías were camped in the mountains near Pilares. They had run out of food and decided to ride to the Neville Ranch and rustle some cattle, according to Miles. On arriving, they saw the destruction wrought by the previous raiders, along with the bodies of Glen Neville and Clara Castillo. The Villistas spotted several head of cattle in a nearby corral and rounded them up and rode away.

About an hour after the raiders departed, cavalry Troop G, consisting of thirty-one men and led by the now Major Henry H. Anderson and accompanied by Adrian Castillo, arrived at the ranch. As they rode up, Neville called to them and was invited to come forward. Minutes later, they found Glen Neville. He had been shot in the head and one knee but was still alive.

Ed Neville later remarked that Glen had a wound in his forehead "you could drop a hen egg through" and that he had been beaten badly: "he was black and blue all over his face and head."

It was decided to carry Glen into the house and make him comfortable while his wounds were treated. As Neville and several soldiers entered the house, they were ill prepared for what they found. Clara Castillo was found dead, shot in the head and torso. She was propped up in a seated position in the kitchen. She had been mutilated—her breasts had been cut off and were lying on the floor on both sides of her body. José Castillo, her young son, was standing nearby crying. He suffered a serious head laceration. Two other Castillo children were huddled together, crying, in a far corner of the kitchen.

When the raiders were finished with Glen Neville and the Castillo woman, they had turned their attention to looting the house. Neville said everything in the house "was torn upside down, scattered all over, and everything gone." The only thing the bandits left were some bedsteads and wooden trunks that had been emptied of their contents.

Though Neville and the troopers did what they could for Glen, they were not equipped to deal with the severe head wound. He died at 6:00 a.m.

A subsequent military report confirmed that a number of the Neville Ranch raiders were either residents of Porvenir or had relatives slain by the Texas Rangers in that town. Others had their homes destroyed later by the US military. At least one of the raiders had worked for Neville on his irrigation project.

The consensus of researchers is that the motivation for the raid was vengeance for the atrocities at Porvenir. The Neville Ranch was selected as a target because, it is presumed, that it was the closest and most convenient. In contrast to the Brite Ranch raid, Neville had little to steal so robbery, though it occurred, was ruled out as a primary motive. The killing and mutilation of Rosa Castillo seemed unnecessary and is more difficult to explain. Author Glenn Justice suggests that this act, along with the battering of Glen Neville, "appear to be acts designed to terrorize those living on the Texas side. . . ."

When it was light enough to search for tracks of the raiders, the troopers found the trail of a great number of horses and men. It led from the Neville ranch house toward the Rio Grande. Several barbed wire fences had been cut to allow the raiders access to the Neville Ranch property.

On reaching a point near the river where the raiders crossed back into Mexico, Anderson was determined to pursue but decided to await some reinforcements. Word was sent to Marfa where Colonel Langhorne readied cavalry Troop A, a total of ninety men. From Marfa, the cavalrymen, along with their mounts and gear, as well as some extra mules to serve as a pack train, rode cattle cars to the tiny village of Valentine in Jeff Davis County. From there, the troopers saddled their horses, loaded their gear, and struck out across the desert and mountain countryside toward the Neville ranch house, arriving at 3:00 p.m. Among the cavalrymen were a handful of competent trackers as well as a contingent of experienced machine-gunners.

All was in readiness. The US Army once again was on the brink of entering Mexico on yet another punitive expedition.

Following the raid on his ranch and the death of his son, the life of Ed Neville took a dark turn. A short time after the incident, Neville sold his ranch and moved to Marfa where he operated a cafe for several years. He sought for and received an appointment as a Special Texas Ranger, and in this capacity undertook to hunt down and kill Mexicans he suspected of being participants in the raid. He had a small black notebook in which were listed sixty names. With assistance from one or more other Texas Rangers, Neville would search for these men at night, an activity that occupied him until he passed away in 1952. According to one of

Neville's daughters, most of the names in the book had a line scratched through them.

It is believed that many, if not most of the Marfa residents were aware of Neville's night hunting activities, but so strong was the fear of Mexicans living on both sides of the Rio Grande and so palpable the racism of the time that his actions were not only tolerated, but encouraged.

CHAPTER SIXTEEN

The Attack on Pilares

ON THE EVENING OF MARCH 26, 1918, THE DAY AFTER THE NEVILLE Ranch raid, Cavalry Troop A crossed the Rio Grande to hunt down the malefactors. The trail of the raiders, who apparently did not anticipate pursuit, was plain and easy to follow. After crossing a low range of mountains named the Sierra Pilares, they set up camp for the night at the T. O. Ranch near Alto Puertain in the Mexican state of Chihuahua.

Before dawn the next morning, the cavalrymen were mounted up and back on the pursuit. The trail snaked back through the Sierra Pilares and headed directly toward the Mexican town of Pilares. On arriving at a high point about two thousand yards away from which they could view the town, they saw that it consisted of no more than twelve to fifteen poor jacales and adobe dwellings. The town appeared quiet, and the troopers advanced.

By this time the raiders either had knowledge of the military pursuit, or had made plans to prepare for such an event, for when the cavalry troop was eight hundred yards from the village (one account says 250 yards), rifle fire erupted from several of the dwellings and from atop a high ridge just beyond the town.

Following the barking of orders from officers and sergeants, a firing line was quickly established and the machine gun squad deployed. The staccato firing of Browning automatic rifles filled the air. Then, the remainder of Troop A charged the village.

On spotting the cavalrymen bearing down on the town, many of the residents, mostly women and children, fled from their homes and toward the relative safety of the nearby mountains. Seeing how vastly outnumbered they were, several of the Mexican riflemen stationed in the town also began to retreat. In moments, Pilares was aswarm with mounted troopers who suddenly found themselves in the midst of a fierce gun battle.

The riflemen who had fired upon the soldiers mounted up and rode away. Troopers took up pursuit, chasing some of them a dozen miles or more into the mountains. By the time the soldiers had reassembled back in the village, they determined the total count of the dead at thirty-three. Eight more were wounded. Only one trooper was killed: Private Carl Alberts was shot from his horse during the initial charge into the village.

Among the dead, one of the bodies was identified as the leader of the Neville Ranch raid—Jesús Urías. It was believed by some that Urías was either a member of Villa's army or a Villa supporter.

With the resistance vanished, the soldiers undertook a search of the dwellings. To their surprise, they found a number of German-made Mauser rifles. They also encountered an impressive store of ammunition, as well as dynamite. They found evidence that the dynamite had been used to make bombs and hand grenades, a tactic successfully employed by Villa's army.

One of the dead men wore chaps owned by Glen Neville. Another was wearing boots that had belonged to the slain son of the rancher. The troopers also rounded up some horses that had been stolen from the ranch.

Quoting from a US Cavalry report, author Glenn Justice noted that "evidence was found linking the dead raiders to the attack on the Brite Ranch, including letters and postcards stolen from Mickey Welch, the mail driver killed at Brite." Several of the dead men wore military-issued dress associated with the Carranzista army. Some researchers have pronounced this as proof that the raid was a Carranzista plot, but no solid evidence for such exists. It is just as likely that the men were wearing discarded military gear.

Following a final search of the dwellings, the troopers burned the town. Only one home was left untouched—it was occupied by an old woman and a child who begged for mercy.

The US cavalrymen may have barely escaped being slaughtered themselves. When a Carranzista general named Murguía, a battalion commander stationed at Ojinaga, some sixty miles downstream, had been apprised of the US troops crossing into Mexico, he quickly organized five hundred of his own men to ride to Pilares to intercede. While the US cavalrymen were setting fire to the Pilares huts, the Mexican troopers were only a few miles away. Alerted to their presence, Major Anderson hastened his own troops back across the border. They arrived back on American soil on the evening of March 26.

Both Mexicans and Americans, residents as well as law enforcement authorities, essentially ignored the existence of the boundary between the two countries and crossed and re-crossed with impunity. The Mexicans blamed the Americans as the source of the difficulties, and the Americans found fault with the Mexicans. It would be many more years, several more killings, and numerous episodes of banditry before a relative peace could be established.

Chapter Seventeen

The Dominguez Clan

Along the international border between the United States and Mexico, small-time bandits from both sides crossed into foreign soil to perpetrate raids, steal livestock, smuggle contraband, and sometimes commit murder. Along the Rio Grande in the Big Bend area of Texas, such occurrences were commonplace and continued for years before law enforcement authorities could put an end to such things. Quite often the raiders were all from some small Mexican village and/or were members of a single family that had lived in the area for generations. Culturally, stealing was often considered by them a fair and reasonable way to make a living.

Then there is this: The Anglo ranchers on the Texas side of the Rio Grande often conducted raids into Mexico to steal cattle and horses and return with them to their own holdings. In many cases, the Mexican raiders were simply retrieving livestock that was initially from them.

One such family associated with border banditry was named Dominguez. During the early part of the twentieth century, the Dominguez family lived on and operated a ranch on the Texas side of the Rio Grande in the Big Bend country. To this day it is still referred to by old-timers in this region as "The Dominguez Place."

As a result of their appearance, it was believed by most that the Dominguez family was descended from the Indians who once thrived throughout this rugged area on both sides of the Rio Grande. They were slight of build, small of stature, and possessed the sharp aquiline features of what author Walter Fulcher described as being "associated with fighting Indians." It has been estimated that there were at least seven brothers, and some claim there may have been as many as eleven.

According to Fulcher, the Dominguez males were "unexcelled as horsemen, mountaineers, and woodsmen, and, though . . . they feared nothing on earth, they had a canny caution and took few unnecessary chances." It is believed that at least three Dominguez brothers, though very young at the time, served as guides for the bandits that raided Glenn Spring in 1916. In 1920, one of the older brothers was killed in a shootout with the Texas Rangers.

Victims of Dominguez family vendettas simply disappeared and were never heard from again. The outlaws left little evidence of their presence and never boasted or spoke of killings. Though they sometimes participated in open gun battles and acquitted themselves well, such was not their style. Evidence for Dominguez clan depredations was so elusive that they were seldom brought to trial, and when they were they were never convicted.

While all of the brothers were involved in rustling, smuggling, and murder, there were three who created the biggest problems for lawmen: Juan, Marceliano (called Marcelo), and Patricio (known as Picho). When not involved in criminal activities, the three found employment on several different ranches in the Texas Big Bend and earned reputations as reliable and skilled cowhands, horse breakers, and ropers. In spite of the fact that it was well known that the brothers were often involved in illegal activities, their skills were highly regarded and in demand, and they always found work when they needed it.

One of the characteristics attributed to the Dominguez brothers was that they were "indifferent to the sufferings of man or beast." Fulcher reported that the young men would ride a horse just for fun until it dropped dead from exhaustion. When one of their horses died from this kind of abuse, they were known to go steal another to replace it.

On one occasion, Juan, along with some friends from the Mexican side of the border, stole a herd of horses. Lawmen were alerted, a posse was formed, and in a short time pursuit ensued. The lawmen followed the trail of the stolen horses through the foothills of a Big Bend range when they noticed that one of the outlaws had headed off in pursuit of a deer. The tracks of the horse and deer were followed into the hills.

What the lawmen found surprised them. Apparently suspecting that a posse was on their trail and not wanting to risk firing a weapon and drawing attention, Juan had apparently ridden the deer down with his mount and killed it with a knife. There were no bullet holes in the hide; the deer had been slashed open. The mortally wounded cervid ran a few more yards dripping blood and entrails before it dropped dead. Juan sliced off the meat he desired and left the rest of the carcass for scavengers.

It has been suggested that under different circumstances, the Dominguez brothers would have been successful robbers of banks and trains or served as leaders of aspects of the Mexican Revolution. Not having access to such opportunities in the Big Bend, and likely not wishing to bend to the rules and regulations of military command, they became efficient smugglers, horse and cattle thieves, and bandits. Their banditry was minor when compared to the James Gang or Butch Cassidy and the Sundance Kid, but so were the targets of their outlawry in this poor desert country in a remote region of the American Southwest.

The Dominguez clan began to gain wider notice during Prohibition. When liquor sales were shut down, the brothers perceived a lucrative market running contraband whiskey from Mexico into southwest Texas towns such as Alpine and Marfa. The citizenry generally resented the notion of Prohibition and customers were effusive in their gratitude for the efforts of the Dominguez brothers.

For the most part, area lawmen were aware of the Dominguez brothers' role in smuggling liquor across the Rio Grande and selling it. They were also savvy enough to know that the citizens were going to acquire strong drink one way or another, so they tolerated the activity.

Unfortunately, while they were running whiskey, the Dominguez brothers continued to rustle cattle and horses from their neighbors. Sometimes when they were on the trail, their packhorses and mules loaded down with contraband, they had little room left over to transport foodstuffs. When it was time to eat, one of the brothers would simply kill and butcher a neighbor's calf for the meat.

The Dominguez brothers also had a bad habit of firing upon lawmen whenever they came upon them, which drew the ire of those who had been letting the brothers go about their business with little interference. With each transgression, the brothers, the welcome contraband liquor notwithstanding, were becoming tiresome in the view of lawmen and citizens alike.

In 1934 Marcelo Dominguez, leading three mules loaded down with contraband liquor, had just crossed the Rio Grande and was making his way to Alpine through the Solitario Hills northwest of Terlingua. On this trip he was accompanied by a partner, a rider who was described as a "dude" who wore high-topped military-style boots and who spoke a clear and precise English. Marcelo spotted some ranch hands gathering cattle not far off the trail and stopped to visit with them. After a short conversation, they all shook hands and Marcelo offered them all a drink. Later, the two smugglers continued on.

Marcelo and the friend reached Alpine, sold their load of liquor, and started back on the trail to Mexico. A short time after Marcelo had completed the sale in Alpine, some nearby ranchers were alerted to his presence. Each of them had discovered several of their saddle horses missing the last time Marcelo passed by on this route, and they were certain he had stolen them. The ranchers approached the county sheriff and informed him of their suspicions. They also told the lawman which trail Marcelo had taken on his way out of town as well as when he would be expected to arrive at certain points along the trail. The sheriff lost no time in contacting federal officials in the area and arranged an ambush at one of the sites indicated by the ranchers.

When Marcelo, his partner, and the empty pack mules arrived at the designated location, the officials showed themselves and demanded that the two men surrender. Marcelo and the dude responded by pulling their revolvers and firing upon the lawmen. During the few seconds of gunfight that ensued, Marcelo was killed from a rifle bullet through his neck. The dude abandoned his horse and fled into the nearby brush, somehow evading the lawmen that fired sixty rounds at him during the escape. Two days later, the dude arrived at a ranch house near the Rio Grande and asked for some food. He had traveled sixty miles on foot.

In time, Prohibition was ended and the smuggling of liquor from Mexico was winding down. A number of Alpine citizens, however, had grown accustomed to the whiskey supplied by the Dominguez brothers and continued to do business with them off and on.

By this time, Picho Dominguez was making the liquor runs from Mexico to Alpine. Not only was he pursued by lawmen from the United States, he somehow managed to attract the attention of the federales in Mexico, likely as a result of his rustling activities. Picho established a hideout on the Texas side of the border at a mountain known by the Mexicans as *Sierra de Matanza*. This translates to Slaughter Mountain. Slaughter Mountain was located eight miles west of Terlingua and not far from the abandoned Mariposa Mine where cinnabar had been extracted from the ground. The Anglos in the area gave this feature the name Black Mesa for reasons that escape logic—it is not a mesa and it is not black.

The name, Slaughter Mountain, has as its origin a circumstance that is far less glamorous than the name suggests. During the heyday of cinnabar mining in this area, a Mexican set up a meat market at the foot of the mountain. He sold goat meat from his herd that he kept in the foothills. He killed and butchered half a dozen goats each day to satisfy the needs of the miners.

Picho Dominguez and a friend named Prejádes Galindo established a camp on Slaughter Mountain. From here, the two men planned and perpetrated a variety of banditry, though for the most part they earned their living selling bootleg liquor. Picho and Prejádes were in league with another Mexican who lived nearby who owned a wagon and several burros. The three men would cut grass, bundle it into hay bales, load the bales into the wagon, and transport it to Terlingua to sell. Hidden beneath the hay, however, were several dozen bottles of contraband whiskey. The bottles were delivered to a Terlingua resident who, in turn, would sell them and divide the profits with Picho.

A number of Terlingua residents recognized Picho, but since he had not stolen anything from them, saw no reason to turn him in. Besides, most of them were his best customers. Problems arose, however, when following a delivery of liquor Picho decided to steal a local rancher's calf and butcher it for the meat. The rancher reported Picho to lawmen.

A few weeks later, a posse of law enforcement personnel, including a Texas Ranger, a US Customs official, and some area deputies, raided Picho's camp at Slaughter Mountain. Following a brief exchange of gunfire, the two outlaws galloped away unharmed. The lawmen entered the camp, gathered up all of the saddles, bedding, camp equipment, and other gear, placed it in a pile, and set it afire. When they departed, they took with them all of Picho's horses and mules that had been left behind by the outlaw.

Picho fled across the Rio Grande and decided to remain in Mexico. Little was heard of him for months save that he was planning to marry a widow and settle down and raise a family.

In 1930, Juan Dominguez was involved in the killing of two men in Texas. Like Picho, he fled into Mexico and was rarely seen north of the border after that. Several months later, however, Juan crossed the river to steal a herd of horses from a ranch he had once worked on. After gathering the animals, he herded them across the river into Mexico.

It was not long before a team of lawmen set out after him. Accompanied by Mexican officials, the posse chased Juan fifty miles into the Mexican state of Coahuila. Disadvantaged by pursuing the bandit in country he knew well, the lawmen neither caught up with Juan nor recovered the stolen horses.

During this early part of the twentieth century, there existed in northern Coahuila an informal organization known as *La Acordaba*, or *'Cordaba* for short. Literally translated, it meant "The Court." In the near complete absence of law enforcement throughout this part of Mexico during this time, the 'Cordaba served as a kind of substitute. In truth, it was a vigilante committee, but it meted out justice to lawbreakers far more often and efficiently than did the federal and state officials. 'Cordaba members would track down and apprehend those who dared to commit crimes against honest citizens, subject them to a trial, and sentence them to whatever punishment deemed appropriate. Sometimes the punishment was execution.

The branch of 'Cordaba that ruled over parts of Big Bend south of the Rio Grande was led by a man named Corona. Corona was respected by most residents, and wielded both a physical and political power in the area. Other members of the court were generally local residents but had skills related to tracking, riding, fighting, and shooting as well as or better than most professional lawmen. In this part of Coahuila, residents were growing as weary of Juan Dominguez and his criminal activities as were residents north of the border. Corona and 'Cordaba decided to do something about it.

Massing a squad of twenty riders, Corona led them into a village where Juan was living. Spotting the approach of the vigilantes, Juan gathered up several of his companions and took refuge in a house. They prepared to shoot it out with 'Cordaba.

Corona and his men surrounded the house and explained that they were there to arrest Juan Dominguez. At this point, Corona realized that there were a number of women and children in the house. Silence followed, and Corona formulated his next move. He instructed Dominguez to send out the women and children because in minutes the vigilantes would commence shooting and setting fire to the house. Moments later, Dominguez and his companions exited the house, their hands raised.

The outlaws were bound hand and foot, loaded into a wagon, and transported to the town of San Carlos where they were to be tried. Because of the reign of terror Dominguez had inflicted on the region's residents, most remained fearful of him and his companions. As a result, none would testify and Juan was released. Before letting him go, Corona met with Juan and explained to him that he must cease his violent ways and stop hurting innocent people. Corona informed Juan that if he were apprehended for similar offenses in the future, there would be no trial; they would simply stand him up before a firing squad and execute him.

Dominguez and his companions returned to their village but paid small heed to Corona's admonition. In fact, Juan bragged to any and all who would listen that he had outwitted the 'Cordaba and would do it again should the occasion arise. Then, he proceeded to take revenge on those who reported him to the 'Cordaba, killing at least two and subjecting others to severe beatings.

On hearing of renewed depredations by Dominguez, Corona, accompanied by a contingent of armed riders, arrived once again at Juan's village. They arrested him and several of his companions with little trouble. Juan and a man named Lorenzo Hinojosa were chained together, placed in the backseat of an automobile, and transported once again to San Carlos. On arriving, the two men were pulled from the vehicle and placed onto horses to which they were tied.

Corona turned to one of the vigilantes and asked him to bring a shovel. When the man asked why, Corona told him he was going to make Juan and Lorenzo dig their own graves.

The two bandits were led some twelve miles to the north to a rough mountainous region near the Rio Grande and just south of the Mexican border town of Lajitas del Sur. Corona sent one of the vigilantes into the village of Lajitas on the Texas side of the river to the trading post there to purchase some coffee. While paying for the coffee, the vigilante informed the trader of the imminent execution of the notorious bandit, Juan Dominguez. The trader, who was well acquainted with Juan and had done business with him in the past, requested that he be able to talk to him before he was executed. The trader followed the vigilante back across the river and along a winding trail. On arriving at the site of the gathered vigilantes, the trader was given permission to only greet Dominguez but was not allowed to talk to him. Following this brief moment of communication, Corona sent the trader away.

As the time for the execution neared, Hinojosa grew nervous and sick and began crying and shaking and begging for his life. Dominguez remained calm. He told Corona that Hinojosa was nothing more than a poor ignorant farmhand and was guilty of nothing. Juan pleaded for Hinojosa to be released.

Ignoring the bandit, Corona stood the two men against a nearby rock and instructed his riflemen to prepare to shoot. One of the riflemen had once ridden with Dominguez and regarded him as a good friend. He grew apprehensive about the execution and fumbled with his rifle, eventually dropping it to the ground. The remaining shooters were likewise troubled by the thought of shooting a man they had ridden with, dined with, and in some cases were related to. Corona, however, was firm in his resolve and his authority was final. At his command, rifle fire resounded throughout the mountains and could be heard at the Lajitas trading post. Juan Dominguez and his companion were dead.

The remaining Dominguez outlaw was Picho. After seeing so many of his family killed by lawmen and vigilantes over the years, Picho decided to give up his life of crime once and for all. He lived out the rest of his days in northern Coahuila working on ranches and living peacefully. As far as anyone knows, he never crossed the border into Texas again.

Another Dominguez brother who occasionally had brushes with the law moved to Texas and found work. His name has been lost as a result of missing records. It was known that, in 1940, he registered for the draft. Following that, nothing was ever heard from him.

The outlaw Dominguez clan, long the bane of residents and ranchers alike in the area, has been gone for nearly a century now and are not expected to return.

Acknowledgments

THANKS TO ARTIST RICHARD "PEEWEE" KOLB FOR THE FINE ILLUSTRA-tions found in this book.

Muchas gracias to C. W. Quallenberg for guiding me through the sometimes confounding maze of computer-related journeys.

Deep gratitude is expressed for my intrepid agent, Sandra Bond, who manages to find a home for nearly every manuscript I send her and who provides her expertise negotiating various projects with television and film producers.

And, as always, thanks to Laurie.

Selected References

Braddy, Haldeen. *Pancho Villa at Columbus: The Raid of 1916*. Southwestern Studies Monograph No. 9. El Paso: Texas Western Press, 1965.
_____. *The Paradox of Pancho Villa*. El Paso: Texas Western Press, 1978.
Brenner, Anita. *The Wind That Swept Mexico*. Austin: University of Texas Press, 1971.
Cano, Tony, and Ann Sochat. *Bandido: The True Story of Chico Cano, the Last Western Bandit*. Canutillo, TX: Reata Publishing Company, 1997.
Daugherty, Franklin W. "Las Vegas de Los Ladrones and the Flynt Gang," *The Journal of Big Bend Studies*, Vol. 3, January 1991, 1–28.
Dodge, Fred. *Under Cover for Wells Fargo*. Boston: Houghton Mifflin, 1969.
Eisenhower, John S. D. *Intervention! The United States and the Mexican Revolution 1913–1917*. New York: W. W. Norton and Company, 1993.
Fulcher, Walter. *The Way I Heard It: Tales of the Big Bend*. Austin: University of Texas Press, 1959.
Gomez, Arthur R. "The Glenn Springs-Boquillas Raid Reconsidered: Diplomatic Intrigue on the Rio Grande," *The Journal of Big Bend Studies*, Vol. IV, January 1992, 97–113.
Harris, Larry A. *Pancho Villa and the Columbus Raid*. El Paso, TX: The McMath Company, Inc., 1949.
Hunter, J. Marvin. "The Killing of Captain Frank Jones," *Frontier Times* 6, January 1929, 145–47.
Jameson, W. C. "Incident at Pirate Island," *True West*, November 1988, Vol. 35, No. 11. 42–44.
Justice, Glenn. *Revolution on the Rio Grande: Mexican Raids and Army Pursuits*. El Paso: Texas Western Press, 1992.
Keith, Noel Leonard. *The Brites of Capote*. Fort Worth: Texas Christian University Press, 1950.
Machado, Manuel A., Jr. *Centaur of the North*. Austin, TX: Eakin Press, 1988.
Madison, Virginia. *The Big Bend Country of Texas*. Albuquerque: University of New Mexico Press, 1955.

Mason, Herbert Malloy, Jr. *The Great Pursuit: Pershing's Expedition to Destroy Pancho Villa*. New York: Konecky and Konecky, 1970.

Maxwell, Ross A. *Big Bend Country*. Big Bend National Park, TX: Big Bend Natural History Association, 1985.

____. *More Tales of the Big Bend*. College Station: Texas A & M University Press, 1988.

Rackocy, Bill. *Villa Raids Columbus, New Mexico*. El Paso, TX: Bravo Press, no date.

Samponaro, Frank N. and Paul J. Vanderwood. *War Scare on the Rio Grande*. Austin: Texas State Historical Association, 1992.

Smithers, W. D. *Chronicles of the Big Bend*. Austin: Texas State Historical Association, 1999.

Sonnichsen, C. L. *The El Paso Salt War*. El Paso: Texas Western Press, 1961.

____. *Pass of the North: Four Centuries on the Rio Grande*. El Paso: Texas Western Press, 1968.

Stout, Jr., Joseph A. *Border Conflict*. Fort Worth: Texas Christian University Press, 1999.

Timmons, W. H. *El Paso: A Borderlands History*. El Paso: Texas Western Press, 1990.

Tyler, Ronnie C. *The Big Bend*. Washington, DC: National Park Service, 1975.

Utley, Robert M. *Lone Star Justice: The First Century of the Texas Rangers*. New York: Oxford University Press, 2002.

Webb, Walter Prescott. *The Texas Rangers: A Century of Frontier Defense*. Austin: University of Texas Press, 1935.

Index

About the Author

W. C. Jameson is the award-winning author of more than one hundred books. He lives and writes in Texas.